THE CALLING OF MY SOUL

True Confessions of a Blue Ray—Empath/HSP

The Wholeistic Healer

BALBOA.
PRESS
A DIVISION OF HAY HOUSE

Balboa Press books may be ordered through booksellers or by contacting:

Balboa Press
A Division of Hay House
1663 Liberty Drive
Bloomington, IN 47403
www.balboapress.com
1 (877) 407-4847

Print information available on the last page.

ISBN: 978-1-9822-2292-5 (sc)
ISBN: 978-1-9822-2294-9 (hc)
ISBN: 978-1-9822-2293-2 (e)

Library of Congress Control Number: 2019902348

Balboa Press rev. date: 03/12/2019

DEDICATION

I would like to take a brief moment in this ultimate soul journey to dedicate some time and energy to the people who have supported my very existence, my life, my struggles, my highs and lows, my spiritual awakening, and my soul's highest evolution.

I dedicate this book to my children who have loved me unconditionally, even in the times when I probably didn't deserve it. You believed in me when I did not believe in myself. You always looked past my quirks, my insecurities, my weaknesses, my human nature. You saved me when you were born more than you will ever know, and you kept me going when I wasn't sure I wanted to.

I can never ever thank you enough for all of the love and lessons I have received from you. I want to let you know that even in my hardest moments on this Earth plane, my love for you never wavered (just like your love for me).

This is for you because some day when you feel like you want to give up, you will think of me and know how hard I fought through my dark times to lead the way for you to do the same. Every time you think you cannot take anymore, you will feel my love for you and know how much I want you to succeed. If I can do this so can you... if I can follow my dreams, so can you. I leave my legacy for you... you are my everything and everything is you. **Daughter**... You are my Sunshine, my only Sunshine. **First Born Son**... don't forget to be a simple man. And to **my Baby** ...The best thing I ever did was believe in me! I believe!! Love always, Momma

TABLE OF CONTENTS

Preface xi

Introduction xvii

Section 1. My Magical Childhood 0-10

Chapter 1   Me and "Them" 1

Chapter 2   My Security Blanket 7

Chapter 3   Friend or Foe 11

Chapter 4   Making Medicine and Maggots 13

Chapter 5   The Beautiful Stranger 15

Chapter 6   The Man with the White Beard 19

Chapter 7   An Unknown Soldier 23

Section 2. The Dramas and Traumas that a Light Worker Faces (Age 11-20)

Chapter 8   Whose dad is it anyways 31

Chapter 9   What was that? 35

Chapter 10   I heard it through the grapevine 43

Chapter 11   The bridge over troubled waters 49

Chapter 12   The Confirmation 55

Chapter 13   Bad Girls Club 65

Chapter 14   The Darkness continues 71

Chapter 15   A second chance at love 73

Chapter 16   Is it just my imagination? 79

Chapter 17   The Journey 83

Chapter 18   White Buffalo 89

Chapter 19 The Magna Carta....................... 95
Chapter 20 Life's Little Surprises 101
Chapter 21 Secrets of an upstairs apt 107
Chapter 22 My Miracle Baby........................111
Chapter 23 The Last Rites.................................117

Section 3. How can I be loved if I do
not love myself? (Age 21-30)

Chapter 24 The Struggle was real...................... 125
Chapter 25 Bleeding Love 131
Chapter 26 The Sinking Ship..................... 139
Chapter 27 Dancing with the Devil.......................143
Chapter 28 My deadly mistake 149
Chapter 29 Playing with Fire.........................161
Chapter 30 Desperado come to your senses 167
Chapter 31 My Ultimate Rock Bottom 173
Chapter 32 Hey Soul Sister..................... 183

Section 4. Waking up from the Illusion (Age 31-40)

Chapter 33 Turning the page..................... 193
Chapter 34 Another devastating blow..................... 199
Chapter 35 New Family Unit..................... 205
Chapter 36 Health Scares 211
Chapter 37 A New Level of Existence..................... 215

Section 5. The Ultimate Becoming of The
Wholeistic Healer (Age 31 and 43)

Chapter 38 The Awakening..................... 223
Chapter 39 The Medium..................... 235
Chapter 40 The Blue Butterfly 241
Chapter 41 Preparing for Dark Night of the Soul 245
Chapter 42 The Twin Flame..................... 251
Chapter 43 The Re-Awakening..................... 261

Chapter 44 The Level Up 267
Chapter 45 The Crossroad 271
Chapter 46 The final strikes 277
Chapter 47 The Darkest Night of the Soul 281
Chapter 48 Finally Healing the Healer 287

Epilogue (in conclusion) 291
Guidance from my Journey to yours 305
Becoming A Butterfly 307
About the Author 309

PREFACE

They say that everything comes in perfect divine timing from God (universe). It has been said that we are all "Divine Sparks" of energy from the creator that are here on planet Earth to complete a specific mission (so to speak) and to learn and overcome specific challenges and purposes. It has also been said that we, as souls plan our re-entrance into the physical existence and that we choose our life before we even get here (maybe even or parents). I have also heard it said that based upon the lessons we must learn, we create certain "Contracts" that we must fulfill in our lives as human beings; and it is our job to do our "Soul work" and figure out what it is we must be working on.

Although I am not exactly sure who said that or why they believe that; I can most definitely say without a shadow of doubt that I know for sure that these are all true to a certain extent in my own experiences and personal reality here on Earth.

I am also not exactly sure if I am different from other people, or if everyone feels that calling of their own soul at some point in their lives; but what I do know is that some people seem to be wide awake to the existence of their soul; while others are completely clueless and resistant to it being a real thing.

Why is that? You ask? Well, from my personal understanding it is due to the level of development that a soul has progressed.

Those of us who are known here on Earth as "Old Souls" seem to be well aware of our multidimensional existence; while those who maybe haven't been on Earth a few hundred times seem to have no knowledge or understanding of who or what they truly are.

As human beings, there are none of us who know exactly for sure what exactly for sure the truth of existence is. None of us know for sure how humans came in to being or how we got here. The only thing we have to go on is our own personal experiences and own personal truths.

When we are lucky enough to have a spiritual awakening, and become "Wide awake", we understand just exactly what it is that our purpose(s) is and why we are here; at least I did.

I have been asked by my divine team to share my amazing journey with all of humanity so that those who haven't realized how much they are needed to change the course of history for Mankind will be inspired to take guided and inspired action on their own journey of love, light, and divinity.

I highly recommend that when you read the stories in this book that you feel the truth in all that you are and let the divine energy and serendipity that you see in my words….. lead you to your ultimate Becoming!

We are all on Earth at a pivotal time in human history and if you are reading this book it is because you have most likely awakened to realize that you are not a human having a spiritual experience… but instead feel you are a soul having a very temporary physical existence.

When I say "temporary physical existence" I do truly mean that exactly. Because if you only knew how many times you have done this song and dance, you would be amazed at all you are!

As for me and my soul; I know for sure that I have been around for at least 27,000 years (According to my guides) and have been to Earth thousands of times.

Each time we come to Earth it is because we have decided that we want to experience all of what we are.

What do I mean by that? Well, when we are not in physical form, we cannot create experiences and therefore we cannot experience what it is like to hold a new born baby for the first time or feel the elegance of the sand between our toes or the rain drops hitting our foreheads....

Because we are only energy when we are not "Physical". We do not always realize that it is a huge honor to be sent to school room Earth to learn and grow and evolve.

According to my guides, we come here to Earth when we want to experience ALL of ourselves!

I was told that when you are not here in the 3rd, 4th, and sometimes 5th dimension you are connected to everything (yes everything) ...... all is one...... everything is in divine perfect order in the 6th dimension and up.

So, you see, to truly experience oneness of our beings, we come to Earth and we are not physically attached to anyone or anything. You come into physical existence with your own divine temple which keeps your life going called your body.

When we choose to do this, it comes along with the forgetting of who and what we are.

It is then, up to each and every single one of us to truly BELIEVE in what we are shown and to follow our signs and synchronicities that will lead us to who we are and why we came.

There are 144,000 souls that were sent to Earth recently to help save school room Earth from the devastation and destruction that has happened over the last 2000 years after the fall of Atlantis.

Remember Dear one... that you are most likely one of the chosen 144,000 souls and reading this book is a wonderful first step to re-gaining your highest consciousness.

This Book is a healing transmission of Heaven to Earth to assist you in remembering that your mission includes helping the divine feminine energy come back into balance to the planet, or waking up the sleepers (the sheeple), or spreading love and peace and unity which will most serve to Raise the Vibration, and to help precious Mother Gaia complete her assigned mission too!

If you have been led to this book it is because you are either at the beginning, the middle, or possible amidst the awakening of all awakenings that will lead you directly to align with your true life's path and purpose.

But somehow the human part of you needed validation that you are not the only one going through what you are going through.

We are in fact all one...... and if you are reading this book... most likely.... You are on the same frequency as me.... You are part of the same soul group as me.... And we probably share a spirit guide and angel.

I was told by my higher Divine Team which includes my higher self that I would lead a mass awakening on Earth...

One that would bring "Many Many Many Many......" to recognize their truth and heal completely in their mind, body, and souls" (My guide's exact words).

I am not the all-knowing Healer .... I am just a humble servant of the light.

Therefore, I am honored to lead when it is time to lead and I am glorified to follow when it is time to follow.

One more thing that I feel is important for you to know; I use the word "Wholeistic Healing" to describe my small local business I created after my awakening and I use the word "Wholeistic" in this book.

Although the word "Wholeistic" is not in any version of the English Dictionaries, it is my personal version of "holistic" which means alternative medicine/healing.

I am honored to be a bringer of "Wholeistic" into existence because first of all I am someone who always strives to be unique and secondly it was in fact my "Whole" journey of healing mind, body, and soul that lead me to my ultimate becoming. It was a "Whole" approach with puzzle pieces put in place that brought me to this moment here today.

So, when you see the word "Wholeisitic" in this book, please know it is my unique version of the English word "Holistic".

Now sit back, relax, and enjoy the flight you are about to take through the bigger picture of our existence....

Open your heart, open your mind, feel your soul and all that you are! You will never regret aligning with the very reason why you raised your hand to come to Earth.

I know that even though I have never really spoken of many of the experiences I have had throughout this lifetime; and even though some of the stories I will tell will be shared for the very first time right here and right now in this book.

I feel with all of me that they will open you up to and awaken things in you that you may have forgotten.... Bring forth more truth and understanding for you about who you are and why you are here too!

I guarantee that when you read this book you will feel as though you are related to me or as though we have had such similar circumstances and maybe have even walked in some of the same shoes.

As you feel this, remember that although this is my turn to lead.... Your turn is coming!

I hope this book lead you into truly hearing the calling of your soul!

INTRODUCTION

I was raised in the Catholic Church and I was taught "Divine Timing" from a very young age. However, the "Divine Timing" that they speak of in the "Christian" religion is only a tiny fraction of what it means to me today.

The dogmatic views on this that I learned as a child have nothing to do with what I feel that phrase means to me at this particular time in my journey as a human being.

Not that I am putting down any religion here; I am simply stating that it is of my opinion from my personal experiences that they never had it completely wrong; they just didn't seem to know the whole story, I guess you could say (Or did they?)

So, what do I mean when I say, divine timing? Well, when I was growing up, I was taught that everything happens in "Divine timing". This was said to me as a child when people were born into the world; this was said to me as a child when people would pass away.

It was the way it was, because it was "divine timing". It was said to be when God had decided that you would be born unto the Earth (and your parents) as well as it was said to be God deciding when you would pass away and go to Heaven, because your duties or mission here on earth were through. You had completed some sort of a level in your being.

Not that I do not believe this to be true, because I most definitely do. But I don't think it ends there.

In fact, I know that it doesn't end there.

There is "divine timing" in every single experience we have here on Earth. I have come to realize that everything we do and every single experience we have here on Earth serves a specific purpose for the growth of our souls.

However, it goes much deeper than that. I have found out, through my life's experiences so far, that this also includes the "divine timing" in which we have that AH-HA moment (as Oprah would say) ... that epiphany... that spiritual awakening... that exact moment when your life flashes before your eyes and you put two and two together and recognize that everything that has happened in your life up until this moment was for a reason.

You know this without a shadow of a doubt! You see clearly why you are here and what you are supposed to be doing with your life.

The day I signed with Hay House to write this book, my publishing manager called me and said "Hi There Wholeistic Healer... Do you believe in divine timing?"

That.... was the moment when I knew it was time for me to tell my story!

Know this; it will for sure happen to each one of us when we are ready to face the complete truth of who we truly are, when we are ready to own up to our mistakes, when we are ready to move forward in life with a much deeper meaning in our hearts and souls. When we are absolutely...positively...truly... ready to do our soul work! It is then that we realize our truth... and its...**all in "Divine Timing"**

I have been following my heart and hearing the calling of my soul for most of my life....

I felt the nudge to write this book at some point in 2016.... But I was told in August of 2017 during an Akashic Records Reading that humanity needs me on a much grander scale.

I was told "you have done your soul work. You have put in a lot of time and effort overcoming dear one. You have always known this day would come and you raised your hand and signed up for this mission before you came to Earth. You have lived and learned and loved and lost and you followed the signs and synchronicities we sent to you again and again and again…. Now Dear one…. we need to let you know… IT' S TIME! It's time to LEAD!

Lead by example and Lead with Love…. Walk through that new doorway of your next level of being and close the old door behind you.

Let go of everything and take a deep breath…. surrender, trust, LEAD.

We grant you the serenity and the courage… you already have the Wisdom for it is within you. Know that if you should choose to take on this mission, you will be Divinely guided and protected like you have never imagined before. You will be taking your stand against all that is not Joy, and Peace, and serenity.

You will be leading your fellow Light Workers to faithfully step onto their unique path and destinies which will then continue this Ascension process that was started on your beautiful planet just a few short years ago….

So, write your first book and it will sell way more copies then you could have ever dreamed of…… people will love it… they will love you! LEAD…. show the way to the light……. Help Bring humanity back to unity and oneness…. help those who haven't found the way yet to feel the light… feel their light! Light the way…. LEAD!"

When I received that message, I knew it was time. I decided to surrender to my mission here on Earth and I know for sure that the vibration of my book will call in those that are on the same mission.

My Magical Childhood 0-10

1

CHAPTER

Me and "Them"

I WAS BORN a love child in the 1970's. The daughter of a divorced single mother of 2 boys; I came into this world exactly 1 month sooner than anticipated. I do believe it was no accident that my birth date was 5/5/75 and I weighed 5lbs. 5oz. at 5:05pm.

In fact, now that I am an adult, I am 5' 5" tall! My 2 children were born on days that break down to 5 and speaking of children, although I only gave birth to 2, I ended up with 5 children who I call mine.

I am someone who has always payed attention to the things that most would look past; but in this instance you can try to look past it, but you cannot deny that there are a whole lot of 5's in my existence and numerology.

5 is the number of change and transformation...... I am certain without a shadow of a doubt that I came here to help create positive change on this planet!

As a baby, in my crib at my mother's apartment; I would see what I realize now were spirits, angels, and universal energy dance around in the room. I can picture it so clearly still to this day; I can still clearly feel that unexplainable feeling that would fill my whole being up when I would see and feel them come.

The feeling I would feel when they were around me still remains today as a way for me to recognize when divine presence is around me.

It is a solid feeling and a complete knowing that you are loved beyond the reaches of the Human mind and that you are cherished above and beyond the realms of what exists here in the physical world.

To this day, I can still recall that as a baby I just seemed to come alive with their presence, I would just light up when I would see and feel "them".

They would come in all colors of the rainbow and seemed transparent at times; however, I do also remember times when I would see them in solid form in shapes like circles, oblong circles, star-like shapes, and even from time to time I would see them in what seemed to be like a Humanoid form.

I know most people talk about seeing angels and they talk about the wings they see the angels come with.

Although I do not completely disagree with this, because I know and have personally witnessed the wings that they speak of.

However, my physical eyes perceived it more like a sideways figure eight which would move and shift and transform as they moved around the room.

I very distinctly remember one of "them" in particular that I would look forward to seeing every time it would get dark. This one was very bright yellow and would have what appeared to be a ring of orange around the outside.

When that one would show up, I would feel as though I was supposed to close my eyes and rest. I t was kind of like an every day alarm clock that would tell my little human being when I needed to replenish and restore.

No matter what, though, I would see them daily. I would lay there giggling in my crib as sometimes if they got close enough to me, I could feel what I can now explain as a sort of wind that would gently blow at my face and tickle my cheeks.

It would sometimes tickle my entire body and I can still feel it as I sit here writing this in this very moment.

As I got a bit older; around 2, as I started to learn how to talk and walk, I would talk about "Them".

Although no one else seemed to understand what I was saying, when someone would ask me who I was talking about, I would simply say "Them".

If someone would ask me who I was talking about, I would say "Them".

To me, they were Them". It was my way of describing all of them!

At 3 years old, my bed was surrounded by "Them" every night. Back then I had a strong knowing that they were my friends and I felt very safe with them by my side.

I know it has been said that we come into this world with spirit guides and angels that watch over us and keep us safe; I can honestly say that since the moment I came here to this planet, I have known that I was highly guarded and truly protected.

I can honestly say that I have very fond memories of the love and care I felt around my bed when the lights would go out at night. I now know for certain that "Them" were my heavenly helpers that there were always many of them surrounding me when I was a baby and young toddler.

Every night when my Mother would tuck me in and then leave the room it was like fireworks watching lights dance around the room. I would giggle and feel completely jolly as they would light up my room and seem to light up my whole being with their presence.

Somehow even though I was that young, I still can picture all of them circling around my bed and as long as they were around, I would drift off into a deep sleep and never felt scared at all.

Besides what I have already shared with you, I guess the best way I can describe in a bit more detail what I saw and felt was kind of what you see when you watch the Tinker Bell movies and you see the small dots of light which then spread out into bigger circles of light and then beside them are what appear to be pretty large orbs of light.

I would know as soon as I saw a light blinking or the moment, I would see the room seem to illuminate with the undying presence of peace, love, Heaven on Earth; that I was supposed to just close my eyes and rest. I still do not know how I knew...I just did.

That was what I was lucky enough to have around me at all times at night in the dark as a toddler.

Sometimes they were colored and then other times just white; but none the less I knew as soon as they arrived each night that it was time for me to drift off to sleep.

Sometimes I would see "them" in public or in the car when I went out with my family back then. I was never fearful of them at all; I always felt so much comfort and love and peace when they were around me.

There was one specific night when I saw "Them" in what seemed to be angelic form.

My brothers and I were spending the night at my Grandma and Grandpa's house on my Mother's side; as we often did. For some reason I was terrified of my Grandma's bedroom and I was placed in her bed to go to sleep and she shut the door after tucking me in.

Her bed felt so cold and lonely to a little girl who was used to sleeping amongst friends and having her Mommy there and I cried for my Grandma to come get me out of there.

She came in and was frustrated with me and sternly told me to "go to sleep!"

She walked back out of the room for the 2nd time and I fussed and cried loudly again because I did not feel safe in the room.

I waited for my Grandma to come in one more time and although I knew she would be mad; at the time it seemed better than laying in that big scary bed in the dark all alone.

As I waited a few more minutes and watched for the door to open and let in a little bit of light; I was instead embraced by the hugs and kisses and warm inviting light swirls on the ceiling.

At first, I watched as one was blinking and then another came in; followed by a few more and before I knew it the whole room was engulfed with "Them" and for the first time (that I can remember) I watched an angel appear in form from out of nowhere.

I saw the bright shining light that radiated throughout all of its being and it appeared to have shooting lights and energy bouncing out from the center.

This angel was pink and orange and as tall as the room; at the time I had no clue what it was, but all I knew was that it was a good thing and somehow, I knew it had come to my rescue.

I laid there as I could feel it sending some sort of essence towards me and as soon as it hit my physical body, I felt immediately calm and safe. I know this may seem silly to some, but it felt a lot like my own mother's energy; it reminded me of my mommy and then suddenly I didn't miss her anymore in that moment.

I still to this day cannot explain the true glory and honor that probably happened in that room in a small town in Wisconsin that evening in 1978.

Looking back now, it was one night where I sure wish I would have been old enough to understand and share my experience; but somehow back then I just knew to keep it to myself.

I will never forget the way it made me feel when the radiance seemed to send waves of peace right through my entire little being. I would lay my weary little head down and listening to the sounds the angel made until I fell asleep.

I could never perfectly explain the sound, other than it was almost like someone was singing in a high-pitched tone. Although it was high pitched, it was comforting and as if it was singing me a lullaby.

Although not a word was spoken there was a Universal language that was not only heard but felt throughout the whole room that evening that still to this day I have never stopped seeing and feeling in my mind.

Just the overwhelming feeling of being cradled in the hands of "God" and being loved so much that you have no other choice other than to just become still and silent. That was the very best rock-a- bye I have ever experienced.

2

CHAPTER

My Security Blanket

SHORTLY AFTER THAT, my Mother met "Him"; the man who would take on the responsibility of raising me the rest of my life; Bill.

For the sake of this book, going forward I will refer to "Bill" as my dad, because he is the only one, I would end up truly knowing in that role.

For the sake of you understanding "Him" let me just say that at that age I called my dad "Him".

When my Mother would ask me questions or be speaking about Bill, I would not say Bill or dad at that age; just "him".

When he would try to bond with me, I would cry to my mother and say, "Him is looking out me!"

I never liked him to look at me apparently and if I would catch him, I would throw myself into a hysterical tantrum and say, "stop looking out me!"

My Mother to this day lovingly recalls the amazing love that Bill had for me back then. She says that she always felt sorry for him because he would try so hard to get me to like him and I was just not having it.

I am sure it most likely came from spending the first 3 years of my life with just my Mom and my 2 older brothers.

It wasn't that I didn't want a dad; but back then I had no clue there was such a thing and so I highly preferred not having one "looking out me"!

It was a matter of time before we moved into his farm house with him and I stopped seeing "them" (my magical angelic friends) after that: at least for a while.

After we were all settled in and living life on the Farm with our new dad, my brother accidentally burned our house down; with me in it. You see my mother had put my brother and I down for naps that day; my brother was 18 months older than me, so he would have been around 4 and I was 3.

After us two kids fell asleep, my mother decided to sneak in a little cat nap herself and so she laid down in her bedroom and fell asleep. My brother must have awoken before anyone else and he found my mother's cigarette lighter laying in the living room on the table.

Back then people smoked cigarette's everywhere; in the grocery stores, in the hospitals, and in the house! So, it wasn't any sort of unusual activity for her to leave her pack of cigarettes and lighter lay on the coffee table in the living room when we went to bed.

Anyway, my brother picked up the lighter and from what I was told flicked it a few times and the curtains in the living room became engulfed in flames.

Back then it was common to have the long heavy burlap curtains that would drape down all the way to the floor. Although they were quite popular back then, little did anyone realize how very dangerous they were in terms of being a fire hazard. So as the living room went up in flames, my mother awoke and called for help.

As the flames started to move throughout the first level of the house, I was sound asleep, directly above the room that was burning fast and furious; as I woke up to people screaming and a man throwing me over his shoulder like you see in the movies; I saw flashing lights all around him and myself.

There should have been no reason on God's green Earth that my savior that day and myself should have gotten out of that fire alive. As I sit here thinking about what I saw, it makes my skin crawl. I watched as he carried me down the steep steps of the farmhouse and pushed his way past the flames that had absolutely taken over the hallway and the rooms on the first level. I could hardly breathe, and it felt like my lungs were getting smaller and smaller with every gasp and every scream my little being would let out. I watched as the flames were completely surrounding him and I and looking back, it was truly a miracle that we got out. I saw with my own eyes how when the flames would try to take over and trap us suddenly there was a shower of golden light that would seem to shield us from being burned alive.

In those horrific and terrifying moments I was so happy that they showed up. Oh, how I had missed them. Where had they been?

But in those moments while my hero, who was the next-door neighbor who had seen the house in flames and ran down the street to help. A true and real good Samaritan who saved my life that day more than he will ever realize.

I screamed, "My silkie!!"; which was my favorite blanket with silk around the edges (AKA my security blanket) that I absolutely had to have in order to sleep for comfort at that age.

I watched as he set me down safely outside and ran back into the house to rescue my silkie. I still do not know how he did it other than the knowing that he did not act alone that day. He was very much assisted by higher forces of the Universe. I watched as he handed me my favorite blanket and turned around and went in the house one more time to rescue a cat we had at the time. I heard my brother screaming "please, help our cat! She is in there!". And just like in the movies where you see someone get out just in time before the building collapses; that is exactly what I saw that day. Perfect timing! Everyone was out and safe and happy.

I do not remember a whole lot after that; other then I still recall the feeling I had inside when I knew that we were all safe. The next thing I knew, we were standing outside watching the firemen spraying water everywhere and while they did, I saw "Them" all around me, all around the house, all around my Mother and my big brother.

I realize just now as I type this that ... on that day going through that extreme situation was the day when I first started feeling like the bottom was going to fall out from underneath me.... that was the day when trauma started to become the way of my life.

It would last for many years going forward. That was the first time in this lifetime that I had my security (and my security blanket) taken away from me unexpectedly; it was the first of many traumatic experiences, which would lead me to a life of trying to find Heaven again amongst all that hell on Earth for the first 30 some years of my life.

So as a metaphor I am going to say this; even though I had my home and everything I owned and knew taken from me in an instant.... I still got to keep my "Security blanket". I see it now, but then... not so much. I was always blessed and watched over and protected. Life is like that for everyone if we just look at the bigger picture!

After the fire, my family was lucky enough to have a home to temporarily move into; because my dad's family had a family member that had passed away and his home was empty and for sale at the time. (Imagine that...Divine Timing).

3

CHAPTER

Friend or Foe

ONCE WE MOVED into that temporary home for a while, I started to see my angelic friends (AKA Them) around my bed at night again. My room would light up with joy and love when the lights went out. I was absolutely surrounded.... And this is the first time I have ever spoke of this!

One night, after I was tucked in, I was encircled with the flashing lights and angelic friends and fell asleep. I was awakened by a noise I couldn't feel good about. I looked over the side of my bed and there was a pig in my bedroom. I screamed for my mom, as the pig starred at me. I do not think I had ever been so scared in my entire life at that point.

My mother came in and carried me to her bedroom... I pleaded with her to "Get the pig out of here!"; but she simply told me I was imagining it and that there was not a pig in the house....

Although she couldn't see it, I know for sure I did not imagine that! I know what I saw, I will never forget it!

As she carried me down the hallway towards her bedroom; I watched behind her as it followed us. I screamed and cried and begged my mom to hurry up and run so it didn't bite her. She continued to tell me it was just a dream and that we were ok; there was no pig in the house.

As we reached the doorway of her bedroom it looked up at me and I saw its eyes shine bright red and then fade to black and then suddenly it just dissipated as we entered my parent's room.

My Mother laid me in the bed where my dad lay sleeping. At that point I knew that as long as I was not laying on the outside of the bed, I would be safe for the night tucked away between my mom and dad and therefore no harm could come to me.

I did notice that when that pig was present, my "friends" weren't there (or at least I didn't see them).

To this day, I still am not sure the meaning of any of that. I just know that the incident is one of the significant memories I have, and it was when I first started to realize that I could see things that others couldn't. I also started to realize that I could feel things and just knew things that others didn't. I mean I felt darkness with that pig; but still cannot explain it!

It was not too long after that, that I started to see and feel "dark" and/ Or "Negative" Spirits in houses and buildings and without even trying to I could see them hanging on and attached to people as well.

I would feel what others felt when they came into my path and without even trying, I could think about "Clearing" that icky stuff off people and I could see it leave when it saw me.

I was not sure at the time why or even how; but I had a knowing that I had power behind me that could ward off the creepiest and yuckiest of boogie men!!!

At the time, however, I just knew to keep it to myself.

CHAPTER

Making Medicine
and Maggots

AS A YOUNG child, I absolutely loved going into the woods by myself and making what I would call "medicine". I would pretend I was a Native American Indian and I would pick leaves and barks and pretend that I was going to heal my stuffed animals with it.

I can't exactly explain it in my human mind, but when I was in the woods "medicine making", I could feel a presence with me.

The "presence" was a male Native American and then sometimes there would be what kind of appeared to be a pioneer looking little girl who would walk around the woods too.

The funny thing is at the time, I didn't think anything of it. I never talked to either of them or anything like that; but somehow, I knew when they were around me. I saw the little girl more often. It was like she was walking through the woods just playing and looking for plants and twigs like me. I didn't want to disturb her journey and really wasn't too worried about her. One day she was hiding behind a tree and jumping out, giggling. I felt like she was a nice girl, but I didn't know who she was or why she was hanging out with the Native American man. I was too busy in my own world to connect to it though.

I was on a mission to "Heal" my stuffed animals from all their ailments and woes.

If my mother is reading this, it might be the very first time she hears this story and thank goodness I am in my 40's so I don't get grounded!

I used to bring the medicines, which I formulated with all kinds of leaves and barks and mud and sometimes even smarties candies that I would mash up; into the house and up the stairs to my bedroom where I had a doctor's office all set up and the stuffed animals were lined up on chairs in the waiting room for me to give them their treatments!

I would call them in, one by one, give them the once over and diagnose them and then give them the medicine I had just gone in the woods and made.

I would give the really sick ones what I called surgery and that would entail me cutting a hole in their mouth, so I could stuff the plant medicine into them to heal them fast!

Until one day, I was getting ready to go to bed and I grabbed a teddy bear to sleep with and he had maggots crawling out of his mouth from the rotted "medicine" I had been giving him. That was the end of that!

Little did I know at the time that plant medicine making was truly imbedded in my whole being and I am certain now that I have done it in many lifetimes.

5
CHAPTER

The Beautiful Stranger

I DIDN'T KNOW it at the time, but I was quite lucky to have the self-reliance / self – entertainment skills that I did; because life started to get very hard for a long time around the age of 7.

It started out once again with a traumatic fire that would take down the barn on the farm we lived on (yes, the same farm that the house burned down with me in it just 4 years earlier). I will never forget that day because although it was Labor Day and was intended to be a wonderful day of hanging out with family and cousins…. I watched as flames blazed out the kitchen window that morning.

My mom had been standing there washing dishes and I thought I saw fire; I said, "Mom look" and she screamed…

The next thing I knew there were people and fire trucks everywhere; people who had been passing by had stopped in to help, and it was the first and only time I ever saw my dad cry.

Why? You ask? Well you see my 2 brothers were in the barn when it went up in flames; as they were doing chores.

My youngest brother was found shortly after that, but my oldest brother was no-where to be found.

In an amongst all of the chaos that was happening, a beautiful woman walked into the house and asked me if I was ok.

I started to cry and said, "I am scared!" …

"Of course, you are beautiful girl, but you know what?" she said in an angelic voice to me.

But before I could answer her, she took my hand and lead me to the living room couch and sat me on her lap and said.

"Do you believe in God?" and I said "Yes, I think so."

Then she asked me "Do you believe in angels?' and I said, "I don't know really what they are, but I think so."

She smiled so lovingly at me and she had such an energy about her that to this day I still cannot explain. She held me with so much love and compassion, that even now as I write this, I am still figuring out exactly what happened in that moment. but....

She told me to put my hand over my heart and so of course I did and then she said, "Do you feel that?" and I said "Yes! That is my heartbeat!!! I feel it!!!"

She lovingly smiled even bigger and said, "Anytime you ever feel scared, remember you can place your hand over your heart and ask God to be with you; when you do this, your guardian angel will know you need love and be there right away!"

In that moment, she seemed so celestial and even at such a young age, I didn't know what she was saying. But, yet somewhere within my being I knew exactly what she was saying at the same time!

I also remember that right then and there, I placed both of my hands over my heart and asked God secretly to myself if my oldest brother was going to be ok.

It wasn't even 15 seconds after I had the thought that the lady placed her hands on my cheeks and said "Oh beautiful, lovely little child; your brother will be just fine. He is safe, I promise you!"

I was so shocked. How did she know that I had just asked that in my head to God?

Did she hear me? Maybe I said it outload? I was so amazed!

The Next moment came by quickly and I heard my baby sister screaming in her playpen and then I realized the chaos that was going on all around us.... She told me to go pick my baby sister up and hold my hand over her heart too. I ran over and did exactly as she had asked and I turned around to see if she was approving of my loving embrace that I then turned around and gave my sister.... But the woman was gone.

Now that would end up being the first time I walked and talked with someone that no one else saw or heard; but it certainly wasn't the last.

As soon as my baby sister was calmed down, I embraced my Mother and told her that I knew my oldest brother was going to be ok. She said, "I hope so sweetie" and I replied with "I know so Mom!".

Very shortly after that, my dad came running in the house with my oldest brother in his arms and we all cried and felt thankful that we were all alive and well. The barn was a complete loss, but just as the lady told me, my brother was safe and ok!

To this day, I truly believe that beautiful stranger must have been my guardian angel; I always wondered though if she was one of the "Friends" that would be in my room at night. Her energy felt so familiar to me.

That day I had the overwhelming feeling that I was an Earth angel. or that I was very much different and unique. I always had angelic presence around me in sort of a "Protection" ... as a young child I knew this (not sure how) ... but I guess looking back at it now; I just thought it was like that for everyone!

Either way, I was blessed that day not only to have been calmed and loved in the eye of the storm that was happening.... But I also learned a lifelong skill that I use even today!

Like I said earlier, if I truly look at it; every single trauma had significant blessings. I was always protected and guided my entire life. It just took me a very long time to recognize this (I think I am truly recognizing the level of this protection as I speak on a whole deeper level).

6

CHAPTER

The Man with the White Beard

SINCE WE ARE talking about the guardians and guides that are seen and unseen to us all here on Earth, I know for sure now that I have had many of them walk this life with me.

How do I know? Well, because as a child, there were countless times when I would see who I then called "the man with the white beard".

This man would seem to show up everywhere I went. I would see him in crowds, I would see him standing alone, I would see this man …. what seemed like everywhere from as far back as I can remember until around 10 or so years old.

I guess, just like everyone else that you see when you are a child who lives in a small town; I never thought anything of it really; It seemed like I saw him everywhere.

He would always smile and wave in public and I guess since I didn't know any better, I unknowingly thought everyone else could see him too and that he must have been a popular guy in my hometown.

Until one night, when I saw him standing outside my living room window and that changed everything, I ever had thought about him.

It was a Saturday evening and my parents left for a night out with friends to their favorite hangout spot.

All of us kids were home under the care of my oldest brother and I had a friend spending the night.

My best friend and I had decided to put a movie in the VCR and make sleeping bag beds on the living room floor; with popcorn and soda pop of course.

For some reason the movie kept stopping and then we would have to rewind it and start it over (It was the strangest thing….).

So, for the fourth or fifth time, I got up to re-start the movie and as I stood up I had a clear view of our front lawn and there he stood, right outside the window… the man with the white beard!

I panicked and ran (if you can run in a living room) as fast as my little self could and buried myself underneath the blanket, I had been previously been cuddled in… covered my whole entire face and tried to catch my breath.

I could hardly breathe, and I could most definitely not speak for a moment (or for what seemed like an eternity to me at the time).

My friend, surprised and probably a little jilted herself from my reactions repeatedly kept asking me "What's wrong?" and "What happened?" and "Are you ok?"

But no matter how much I tried, I couldn't speak to answer her, I had myself safely tucked under the blanket just shaken to my core.

Eventually when I caught my breath, I asked my friend "Did you see the man with the white beard outside the window?"

She exclaimed "NO…. what man?" as she ran to the couch and covered up too.

I replied "The man with the white beard! I see him everywhere I go it seems. I am sure you have seen him in town too. I know you would know him if you saw him. I think he is from Lodi, but why is he standing outside the window?"

She was speechless and all we knew was we were scared!

I called my mom at the tavern they were at with friends and begged them to come home.

I swore to them that there was a man standing outside the living room window and that I was not making it up!

My parents came home but were very upset with me. To their dismay, of course there was no man standing anywhere around the farm.

My dad walked around the whole premises and came back into the house and called me into their bedroom.

He said "There was not really a man was there? Why did you make up a lie like that?"

I replied "NO... Dad, there really was, I saw him!"

He sternly said, "Now if there was truly a man here and you saw him, then you won't be afraid to go to the police station and report this, right?"

I excitedly exclaimed "Yes! I truly saw a man outside the window and YES! I WILL go to the police station and report it. I promise I am not making this up!"

I could tell he was very frustrated with me and although I knew I was not making it up (I knew what I saw); at the same time, I also knew there was no way for me to prove that it happened. And so as not to upset my parents any more, since they had ended their night with their friends early; I backed down and said "Well maybe I imagined it, I don't know. I am very sorry!"

Even though, I very much knew for sure I was not lying, that was one of the many times throughout my childhood and early adult years, I would back down on my story as to fit in or please others; or simply to not get in trouble like in this case.

That was also the last time I saw the "Man with the white beard" for many years.

Growing up very different from everyone around you, but not ever being able to explain it to yourself or anyone else for that matter is not an easy task!

In fact, I spent so many days and nights as a child wondering if I was making things up or if I was lying; since everyone around me always seemed to think I was.

Even though I knew I was not and I knew my intentions were always pure and that I was truly speaking my truth….

For some unknown reason to me (at the time), others just couldn't seem to understand that about me. Others just couldn't seem to see and know me for who I was and only I seemed to understand this.

Eventually, I started to truly hold everything in and not share, because I didn't want anyone to think badly of me. I just wanted to be loved and accepted in my family and in the community.

I started to shut down a lot after the man with the white beard outside the window incident.

7
CHAPTER

An Unknown Soldier

ABOUT 3 MONTHS after I saw the man with the white beard standing outside the living room window, I had another significant experience that was an important puzzle piece that molded me into the "medium" I am today.

It was a school night and back in those days, we did not have internet or cell phones. For entertainment at night in my bedroom upstairs in the old farm house I had pencils and paper and I would write stories and poems and draw sometimes.

That particular evening, I put my pencil down because I felt an eerie presence in my room.

I tried my best to shake it, but no matter how hard I tried to write and focus on forming sentences; I just couldn't seem to sit still.

I can't explain it, I just felt like someone was standing over me watching me. Yes, I had felt this sort of energy or presence before, but not ever while I was alone in my room. This sort of thing would typically happen in crowds or when I would go to bed at night in the dark.

This was significant. This was something new that I hadn't felt before. I just couldn't place it.

I continued to look around and eventually as I put my pajamas on, I just knew someone was in my room.

I turned off the lights and laid in bed with the covers completely over my head as usual so that whoever or whatever could not see me or touch me for that matter.

Those days, I was terrified of the dark. It had been years since my "friends" were around my bedside at night and oh how I longed to feel them in that moment.

I always tried to sleep with my little lamp on in my bedroom so that I wasn't in the dark; but my dad was a stickler about electricity back then and we had old wiring in the farm house so when he came up to go to the bathroom before bed, it was almost always guaranteed he would come in and turn my lamp off. That particular evening was no exception.

It wasn't like I felt that the presence was bad or evil; it was more like something new and the unknown was super creepy to me that night.

I finally fell asleep at some point and like usual, I awoke in complete darkness. I rolled over half asleep and out of the corner of my eye, I saw something strange.

As much as I tried to keep my eyes away, out of absolute fear; at the same time, I couldn't help but look.

I turned my head and there at the end of my bed, clear as day, I saw a soldier standing there looking at me.

He was wearing full United States Army Uniform, hat and all. Even though at the time I had no idea what that meant, none the less that is what I saw.

He raised his hand to his forehead and gave me a salute. My heart stopped, and then pounded and I tried my best to not move. I think I thought if I laid still, he wouldn't see me.

I tried not to breathe as I saw him sort of dissipate and vanish into thin air it seemed.

After he was gone, I laid there very still; terrified to move but yet I felt safe at the same time. I still cannot explain in human terms how I felt that night.

I had about 2 more hours until daylight by this time and I did not want to go back to sleep. I laid there looking out the window just in awe of what just happened.

What did this soldier want with me? Why was he watching me? Is that what I was feeling as I was in my bedroom earlier in the evening?

Amongst others, these were questions just running through my mind over and over and over.

The real question at that point though was what in the world is going on with me? Why is this happening to me?

I guess the most important question I had as daylight finally hit and I got out of bed and went downstairs by my family was…. Do I share? Or.. Do I keep this to myself?

I still had the man with the white beard incident very fresh in my being and that experience was not reciprocated very well at all. I sure didn't want anymore rejection. Maybe I was making this up? Maybe I dreamed this?

Either way, my mind was spinning that morning. I walked into the kitchen and at the table for breakfast was my parents and siblings.

I sat down and grabbed the box of cereal; attempted to pour myself a bowl and looked up to see everyone staring at me.

"What?" I asked as I realized this. My Mother spoke up "Are you ok? You look pale?"

"Yeah, Im fine!" I replied.

After a few minutes my siblings were all gone from the table and it was just my parents and me. I wondered if I should say something and then I thought "go for it".

"Mom?" I said.

"Something happened to me last night and I am scared." I explained.

My Mother looked up from the newspaper she was reading and asked "What happened?'

"Well, I saw a soldier standing at the foot of my bed in the middle of the night!" I blurted out. It came out like word vomit. Just came out.

I saw my dad quickly put his paper down and look at my mother and say "Did you tell her?"

"Tell me what?" I asked

My mom quickly said "No, I didn't".

"Tell me what?' I asked again, but they didn't seem to hear me.

"What's going on? Please tell me?" I begged.

My dad gives me a questioning look and says "Well you know a soldier died in your bedroom during World War I."

I was absolutely stunned. I could not breathe for a moment. I was trying to wrap my head around this.

"What? When did this happen? Who?" I cried out for more information.

In that moment, I was so. freaked out, because I knew for sure right then that I sure did not make this up, I did not imagine or dream this. I knew from my dad's words that this truly did happen.

I was also so excited because at that moment I also thought to myself. Now maybe they will believe me about the man with the white beard!!!

Just when I felt like I finally belonged and finally was on the same page at everyone else.

My dad said "Well, I am sure that one of the boys or someone told you about the soldier and that is why you imagined it!"

I could feel my whole spirit sinking. I could feel myself shrinking. I felt so deflated once again. At that point it would not matter what I said; they were not going to believe me.

I tried to argue my point anyway though and did my best to get him to understand that I truly did not know anything about this until this morning.

But I also knew that at the same time I would forever be creeped out alone in my bedroom not. Great!

Eventually, for quite a while, I got discouraged from sharing; due to the lack of support I would receive. I do not think that others were intentionally trying to put my light out.. they just truly couldn't see or hear or feel the things I did.

However, there were friends of mine who did share in the mystery with me, but they didn't want to be made fun of, so they would not speak up for me.

But every single time someone ever told me I was a liar or that I was "Imagining" it; somewhere deep within my being, I knew that they just couldn't understand me; even though I didn't know why or how at the time.

The best part of seeing the soldier stand at the foot of my bed was that the very next night, I started to feel that wonderful and loving protection presence around me again when I went to bed.

Every single time, going forward, I would feel all alone, it wasn't long before I would feel and see my "Friends of light" gather around me (sometimes it would be in my dreams). Somehow, I knew it was Heaven reaching out to help me and to support me (I don't know how I knew, but I just did).

The Dramas and Traumas that a Light Worker Faces (Age 11-20)

8

CHAPTER

Whose dad is it anyways

ABOUT A YEAR after the white bearded man made his last appearance and the Soldier made his first appearance (I eventually learned to accept the soldier and co-exist with him) in my childhood, I accidentally found out one day that I had a different biological Father then my brothers had.

I will never forget that day as my brother and I had gotten into a fight; and as we went back and forth with the usual put downs between siblings who are engaging in battle of the wits; I belted out "You aren't my brother anyway!" …

He came back with "Yeah I know! You don't even have the same dad as us! Your dad was mom's boyfriend and he was mean!"

I will never ever forget the feeling I had in the pit of my stomach as I yelled out, "IM TELLING!"

My little heart was on fire and I ran to my room, laid on my bed and thought "My brother is so mean. He is the one who is mean. Why would he say that to me?"

I did some deep thinking and thought… "You know, I did always wonder why I had blonde hair and everyone else had black hair. I wondered if there could possibly be a chance; but repeatedly reminded myself that my mom would never do that to me.

Several hours later my Mother came home from work and I ran down those stairs... I wanted to be the first one to greet her, so I could tell her how awful my brother had been to me and how terrible it made me feel that he said such a horrific thing to me!

She walked in the door and I immediately called out, "Mom... my brother told me that I have a different dad then him. He said that my dad was your boyfriend and that he was mean!"

As I spoke, I saw the expression on her face and I knew without her even saying a word that something was wrong...

She stopped me dead in my tracks and said, "We need to talk!"

I could never explain in my human mind the feeling I felt in my entire being in that moment.

"Who was I?" "If I am not a part of this family, then what family am I a part of?" "Maybe my dad is like me and will save me from these people who do not understand me?" "Can this be?" "I already do not feel like I fit in here, now where I will fit in?" are just a few of the things that went through my head in those few moments of silence...

My mom set down her purse and said, "Come with me." And all I kept thinking as I followed her to her bedroom where we would sit on her bed and my life would forever be changed was... "This cannot be real!"

As she sat down on her bed and patted her hand for me to come sit too, I sat in wonder. She explained to me that this was not the way she wanted me to find out but that yes this was true.

She let me know that the man that I had been going with on weekends with my brothers was their Father and when she had me, he agreed to take me too, so I would have a family to belong to.

I was given his last name just like my brothers so that I would not be singled out. She then told me that she met my Father through her Father (my Grandpa) because they worked together as mechanics.

She told me that she wasn't sure where he was and that if and/or when he ever wanted to meet me, then she would surely let me know.

I sat there, shattered to my core. Feeling so lost, broken, alone, and embarrassed. I think I felt every single emotion there ever was to feel as my whole life as I knew it had all be a lie.

I was a lie! I was a big fat lie!!! No wonder I didn't fit in, no wonder people didn't understand me. Now I know why nothing makes sense... Because I don't belong here!

I wondered if any of them were truly my family. Was she even my real Mother?

Although I felt so alone, I knew somehow that everything would be ok. I knew somehow that I had to just keep walking on my own path and that someday it would all make sense. I do not know how I knew, but I just did.

I know for sure that after that day, I never saw life the same. I started to spend more and more time in the woods by myself; just connecting to Nature and talking to the trees and the plants. They always seemed to love me and greet me.

We had these wonderful Apple trees down in the lane and I would sit underneath them for hours and just think. I would feel a heavenly presence around me that would without words tell me that I was ok and that all was well.

I started to daydream about who my Father was and how noble he must be. How awesome he must be. I thought "If I am a really good girl, then someday he will want to meet me and then will want to love me for me."

I would envision how wonderful it would be when I met him, and he came to take me away from this place where I lived and the people I lived with. I thought Maybe he would believe me when I told him that I could feel and see things that others couldn't.

Life got hard for quite a while during that time. My mom stopped coming home after work because she just couldn't deal with everything going on and my dad (who raised me) started to become angry because my mom wasn't around much.

My family that I knew was falling apart fast. No one got along anymore, and my oldest brother ran away.

Chaos and fighting became a daily function. Although I wanted to run away sometimes; I became pretty good at reminding myself to be a good girl so that my "dad" would hear about me and come and save me from the sinking ship that was my life.

With my mom gone a lot and my dad in the fields and out working a lot, I had to take on the responsibilities of being an adult and making dinner for the family and taking care of everyone.

I didn't mind for the most part, but there were times when I would pray that my "real" dad would come and save me from the mess I was living in.

I spent a lot of time either in the woods or with the neighbor kids for the next several years as I didn't want to be home a whole lot.

During the next few years, everyone in the family struggled. No one was getting along anymore, and everyone was angry.

All I knew was that if I did what I was supposed to do, my real dad was going to come save me so no matter what chaos was going on at home I tried my best to stay focused on my goals of getting the hell up out of there asap!

9
CHAPTER

What was that?

THE NEXT SUMMER, I had a friend spend the night and we pitched a tent in the front yard. That night we were going to stay up all night long; because we were cool like that!

As we set up our sleeping bags and pillows and gathered our snacks, I was sure that this would be a night that would not soon be forgotten... and I was absolutely correct!

In fact, it was one of the most magical nights of my entire life up to that point.

She asks me "Do you want to see something?" and of course because I was always a curious and adventurous girl, I said YES!!!

She pulls out a pack of Virginia Slims and smiles and says "I stole them from my mom! Do you want to try one?"

Now I was an adventurous girl, but I also knew that 3 years earlier, my mother had forced me to smoke a cigarette when I got caught playing with hers; so, I wasn't sure if I could do it. Everything in me said No way... But I could not disappoint my friend and so I said "Sure!"

As she lit the cigarette, I sat nervously awaiting my turn.

She begged me to please not tell anyone she had them and of course I was not a snitch and I promised! We pinky swore on it!

I could clearly hear and feel a heavenly presence with me as I put the cigarette in my mouth and tried to puff it without inhaling and at the same time make it look like I was taking a huge hit!

I could hear a voice saying, "Are you sure you should do that?" and I quickly returned the cigarette to her hands, I looked around and saw nothing... not a single thing.

I thought "Hmmm I must be hearing things again," and I ignored the voice of reason. My friend took a big puff and passed it back to me and as soon as I put it back into my mouth, I heard the voice say again "Are you sure you should do that?"

But once again I ignored the voice and continued to be cool with my friend.

As I handed the cigarette back to her the second time, I saw a bright white light behind her head and I mean it was bright!

I called out to her "Holy Cow! Do you see that light behind you?"

She giggled and said, "That is just the light from the Barn!"

I absolutely knew without a doubt that it was not in fact coming from the Dusk to Dawn Barn lights; there was no way!

I said "No, not the barn light, the bright white light behind you! Its above your head now, look!"

She turned around and said "You are seeing things! There is no light behind me, just the barn light... see?"

Although I knew better, and I knew what I saw, due to way too many circumstances in the past where I was put to shame for what I saw, I decided to not push it and I let it go!

I never did share with her what I heard the voice saying said either.

So, we continued to smoke Virginia Slims, eat junk food and laugh and talk about which boys we thought were cute at school for the rest of the night.

Eventually, we fell asleep and the next thing I knew, she woke me up screaming.

"Oh my Gosh!!! Look!"

Before I could even think of looking, I saw very bright lights! I sat up and said, "What is that?"

She exclaimed "I don't know but it is up in the sky! Look over there!"

We both flopped on our bellies held up by our elbows and peeked out the tent door at the night time sky in all its wonder and glow!

I will never forget what I saw that night.; a huge circular object which flashed and projected brilliant bright lights of all different rainbow colors.

It spun around, it danced in the night sky and it hovered over the cornfield across the street from my house.

As we lay there in shock and in awe and in wonder of what we were seeing, I asked her "Umm...you see that too... right?"

She had a hard time speaking and said "Yes, what is that?"

To which I replied, "I have no idea, but could it be a UFO?"

My friend reached out, grabbed my hand and said "yes... I think it is... but no one will believe us!"

We watched as this thing raised up and then came down and almost landed; it swirled and spun around for what seemed like an eternity; but in all actuality was probably only 5 minutes!

As it raised up for the last time and disappeared into the darkness... We both agreed that we would keep it a secret forever since we didn't want to look or seem like we were losing our minds!

Until the next morning when her mother came to pick her up from the sleepover and she asked if I wanted to come to their house too.

I happily went with and we both jumped in the front seat together of her Delta 88.

Those were the days of being able to squeeze together in the same seat and share a seatbelt in the front.

As we rode down the street and headed down the highway to her house, her mom said "Did you girls have fun last night? How was camping?"

We both looked at each other and giggled underneath our breaths... and in unison we both said "Fine!"

I will never forget what her mom said next "So you didn't see any UFO's last night did you?"

I couldn't believe it, what? How did her mom know our secret?

We both gasped for our next breaths and I watched as my friend looked down at the floor in the car and her mom looked me in the eye for just a second and then back to the road...

Her mom then said "Well the reason I ask is because there was a UFO spotted just outside of Waunakee last night; it has been all over the radio this morning. People are frightened because they have never seen anything like this before and many people called into the radio show to tell their stories of what they saw."

I seriously thought my eyes were going to pop out of the sockets... that's how huge they were opened!

As we both sat in silence, because we had pinky promised to keep it a secret and neither of us wanted to be the one to squeal… Her mom said, "Are you girls ok?"

We looked at each other and grinned and almost in Unison again said, "we saw it too!"

You could have heard a pin drop in that moment when her Mother turned and looked at us both and said "Oh Wow! Did you really? I was just teasing you; but you really truly saw it?"

I got a little bit excited and ahead of myself and said, "Yes and I saw a white light around her head last night too when we were…"

But before anything else came out of my mouth, my friend piped up, interrupted me and said "sleeping! … when we were sleeping!"

"Yes!" said… "Yeah there was this bright light above her head when she was sleeping, and I saw it. She says it was a reflection from the barn light, but I know what I saw!"

By this time, we pulled into her driveway and her mom put the car into park and turned to both of us and said "Girls. Always remember that no matter what anyone else ever says; you are very special girls; more than you will ever know. Some day you will understand what I mean by that! Always follow your heart and never let anyone else tell you who and what you are! Take my advice, because some day you will both look back at this and remember this moment. When you do, know that you are not the typical. Believe in what you see and hear no matter who else doesn't believe you! … ok? Do you girls promise me?"

Although at that age I had no clue what she was talking about, somewhere in my being, it did resonate, and I did understand.

We both shook our heads and promised that we would take her advice. Even though no one around me except the two of them and a few other friends seemed to believe me; I could somehow just feel that my friend's Mom must experience some of the things that I did; I mean how would she know to say that to me? I wondered in that moment if I could talk to her about my secrets and the things, I had become afraid to share?

But then I chickened out and decided to continue to keep it to myself for a while longer!

Little did I know though that the UFO would be the first of many amazing unexplained things I would see and experience in this life!

I had many (many) dreams as a kid of an Airplane crashing in that same field where we saw the U.F.O. that night… but also of a space ship landing in our driveway and me getting on it and going away; only to wake up in my bed, time and time again. The dreams were always the same…

About a week later, my grandparents (My mother's parents) came over to visit and my grandma, who had always smoked as far back as I could remember didn't have any cigarettes.

As she sat on the picnic table on the front yard and handed me my candy, she always brought with her; I asked her "Where are your cigarettes?"

She lovingly smiled and said, "I quit!"

I asked, "How come Grandma?"

She informed me that "Jesus told me it was time to quit, so I did!"

I was very inquisitive and needed details, so I then asked "How did you talk to Jesus? What did he say? How do you know it was him?"

She leaned over and placed her hands on my cheeks and said "When Jesus speaks to us, we just know its him. You can feel it. You just know!"

Well that didn't answer my question, so I went a little further "Grandma?" I said...

"Yes Honey?" she replied.

"Did you dream that Jesus came to talk to you" I asked (Because it happened to me all that time and I was trying to figure out if it happened to her too)

She said, "Sometimes he does, but this time I heard him ask me if I really thought I should be doing that?"

I was floored! Oh MY GOD... that voice I had heard... in the tent... When I lit up! Could it have been Jesus?

How did my Grandma know the exact words that were said to me?

I wondered if I should share with her what happened to me... but since it involved me smoking stolen Virginia Slims from my friend's mother and things that only I could hear... I decided to keep it to myself once again!

From that day on, whenever I heard that voice of reason when I was about to do something I was pretty sure I shouldn't be doing, I just assumed it was Jesus trying to steer me in the right direction (I would later in life find out that my intuition was right on point) and for the most part I would listen; not always though!

I learned eventually that when I followed the feelings deep within my own being it would always lead me to wonderful things!

10

CHAPTER

I heard it through the grapevine

SPEAKING OF MY Grandmother Lillian; that visit where she told me Jesus told her to stop smoking was the same visit where I over-heard my Mother and her talking about my biological father.

I heard my Grandma say, "Well if you think she is ready I will let him know." And I knew they were talking about me!

It was only a few days later that the call came in. I could never forget the feeling I felt when that call finally came in after all of that time, I spent daydreaming and envisioning how he would be and what I would say and how close him and I were going to be as soon as he came for me.

I was deliciously delighted that all of my hard work of being a good girl had finally paid off. I was instantly on top of the world! I guess you could say that I was "over the moon" with excitement!

We had the old-fashioned phones in the old-fashioned farmhouse that I grew up in; that were connected directly to the wall; one downstairs and one upstairs.

Most times when the phone rang, me and my brothers would answer it upstairs; but if Mom already said "Hello" then we would sit on the line and try not to breathe as to not get caught listening in…

This particular time, I got to the upstairs phone first and I heard my Mother say "Hello".

I heard a voice on the other end of the line say "Hello? It's me."

My heart stopped... Could this be HIM? Could it be? I didn't know his name, but I knew that he would come for me!!!

I sat still just listening and I heard her say "HI. I am guessing my Mother told you that she knows?"

He replied "Yes. I was wondering if I could come and meet Our Daughter?"

I will never forget how I felt in that moment... It was like Magic! I just knew he was going to come and rescue me! I just knew it! He did love me and did want me!!!

I then heard my mother say "Sure. When would you like to come meet her?"

He replied, "Can I come next Wednesday?"

She then said "Yes that is fine, I will talk to her. See you then!"

As she hung up the phone, so did I (After her of course so she didn't hear me hang up) and she called my name... up the stairs.

I came running down the stairs and said, "Yes Mom?"

She said, "Come sit down, I need to talk to you!"

As I sat at the kitchen table, I could barely keep my excitement to myself and when I could no longer hold back, I shouted, "I heard the conversation Mom!"

"You did huh?" she said

YES! I heard every word. My real daddy is going to come next week and meet me!"

"Is that ok?" she asked

"yes, I want to meet him Mommy... I can't wait!"

I wasn't sure in that moment if I could hang on for another week though, because I wanted it to happen right now!

The next week went by so slow and although I told my friends at school what was about to go down, I wasn't sure if any of them truly believed me; since some of my stories seemed a little farfetched to other kids my age... I mean, who truly gets to meet their dad that they didn't know about and then suddenly found out about, by accident?

Not a real likely story in a small town like this... So, I just kind of realized that I had to be excited by myself and I was!

I could feel the disbelief when I shared with the other kids in the neighborhood and at school... but it was ok, because I just knew this man was going to come and rescue me!

By next week, I will be in a new home at a new school, living a brand-new life and none of this would matter anyhow!

Maybe the kids at my new school would understand me better? I continued to hold hope that this would be the golden ticket for me to finally belong somewhere... finally fit in somewhere and finally be able to be who I was without others telling me that I was making it up!

OH BOY I couldn't wait one more second... for my new life to begin!

The night before I met my biological father, I prayed that I would be accepted and loved like a girl deserved to be accepted and loved by her "Real" daddy.

I spent hours preparing what I would wear and what I would say. I think I may have slept a total of 5 minutes that night. Just enough to bring in the light of the next day!

I wanted to be a daddy's Girl, and this would be my day of redemption.

When the day came, I got up in the morning and took a bath in our bear claw tub and I think I must have changed my clothes about a trillion more times so that I would look just perfect and he would want me as soon as he saw me!

As promised, around noon a car pulled up and I watched as a Man and a young Woman got out and headed to the door.

I ran down those stairs so fast I am lucky I didn't fall down them!

I hid behind the dining room wall as my Mother answered the door and invited them in.

She called out to me, but I was right behind her and I walked into the kitchen where they were sitting at the table.

We walked into the kitchen and my Mother said "This is your Daughter"

As I looked up, I saw a man who looked just like me in every single facet of being; with the exception of him being a man and me being a young girl. I noticed immediately that he had the same hair color as me. I finally understood why I had blonde hair when everyone else had black! I finally see where I got the deep green eyes from.

Wow, and then I looked at him again in what seemed like the longest moment of time I had ever seen. I was just amazed. He was so handsome and appeared so strong. He wore a flannel shirt, half way buttoned up; just like my dad that had raised me. The only difference is that he had a tire pressure gauge and a pack of Camels sticking out the top of his pocket. My dad that raised me always had a pack of Juicy Fruit and a wrench sticking out of his pocket.

I wondered as I saw this if the two of them would get along.

Just as I pulled myself out of the gaze I had on the man that I had waited endless amounts of time to see; I turned my head to the left just a tiny bit and laid my eyes the most beautiful young woman I had ever seen.

I heard her voice say "Hi there little sister; I am Tammy Jo... I am your big sister!"

And then the man sitting at the table said "and... I am your Father"

Those would end up being the only words I remember from that conversation because I was so enthralled with my New big sister (who was 21 at the time and had told me that I had a 2-year-old Nephew!) and my new dad who was going to come and rescue me from the life I was living!

About a week or so later they came and picked me up and took me to meet my grandparents on that side of the family and a whole bunch of other relatives.

As I walked through the door at my Maternal Grandparent's home that day, I was greeted by two of the most beautiful souls I have ever met on this planet.

My Grandparents greeted me with so much love and welcomed me with so many hugs and kisses.

It was weird because although they didn't know me, and I didn't know them; there was such a strong bond immediately with the two of them.

I saw pictures of myself in frames all over the living room right along side of all of their other grandchildren

It was such a huge family and I wasn't sure why, but besides the immediate and close connection I felt with Grandpa and Grandma; I still felt like the biggest outsider in the world.

They all knew each other and had their whole lives. I was once again the one who didn't really fit in.

I had been here before. I recognized the feeling very well; that relentless tearing of my insides that I felt when I was surrounded by people who I longed to fit in with, but simply was so out of place that there was not a good way to even begin to try and belong.

I did continue to grow a lasting relationship with my Grandparents and I became pretty close with both of them. They would come to the farm on my birthday and Christmas every year and bring me a new sweater. I always looked forward to their visits with me

As for a long-lasting relationship with the man who I had dreamed of being saved by; well, my dreams would come crashing down on me shortly after I met my Grandparents; when the visits I had with my biological father would be a total of about 6 from the time I met him until I was an adult. It just didn't happen; he just didn't come rescue me!

I loved going with him when I did, but we both felt so very uncomfortable and we just didn't know each other. He seemed to just give up after a few times of being with me and I felt very shy around him and didn't know what to say. It was the strangest thing, because I have never felt shy around anyone in my entire life until I met him.

He had many other children and they all appeared to be pretty close with him. He seemed to have a big love for most of them, especially Tammy who was his oldest.

I sure didn't blame him because I loved her the best too! I ended up becoming close with my new big sister instead of my new dad.

11
CHAPTER

The bridge over troubled waters

AS FATE WOULD have it, my big sister Tammy, her husband, and her children eventually moved about 6 miles away from the farm where I lived. I became her babysitter and spent a good amount of my time at her house getting to know my nephews (there were 3 all together).

There were a couple of times when I would be at her house babysitting and my biological father and his wife would come over to visit her or drop stuff off for her boys; but would pay no mind to me being there.

I had to go out of my way to get them to see me sitting there in the room.

I eventually changed my mindset from wanting him to come rescue me to just wanting him to notice that I existed. (to this day it has never happened. It was heart break after heart break just trying my very best to let him see me for who I truly was and not what he thought I was because other kids of his would stain his perception of me out of their own abandonment wounds with him and wanting him to notice them too; it was a losing battle and I eventually had to let him go.)

It was one of the biggest heartbreaks of many I endured but a strong foundation of me being forced to love myself even when no one else seemed to care about me. At the same time as this major heartbreaking was happening, my Mom was still not coming home, and I had to learn to love myself and be my own best support system.

To this day, I still long for him to love me at times; but I also know that it will never happen, it wasn't meant to.

My guides and angels told me once that some people are only meant to bring us here. His soul contract with me only involved donating the sperm that brought me into this world... My best guess is that is probably why he never really felt much of a pull to see the real me; but I truly have no clue how a parent wouldn't want to know and be close with their children.

The circumstances and environment that I was living in during those important years of my upbringing (from about 11 to 17) would end up being the very thing to hold me back from true love time after time; due to the levels of abandonment that were imprinted into my being from the whole situation.

I spent most of my life up until I graduated from high school being lied to and then finding out the truth... but still having no control over any of the outcome.

I never really knew what it was like to have a trusting and complete bond with a parent other than my Mother and even that was jaded after that ...

But Through all the heart break, I always had angels, and spirits around me. Sometimes they were little children that seemed so happy and peaceful. They always seemed to want me to cheer up.

Every time my heart was breaking because things were not good at home and I had lost the daydream of my knight in shining armor that would come save me ... I would hear a voice say, "You are loved child" or "Hold your head high for you know not who you are".

At the time it meant nothing to me, as I was just trying my best to get by day to day.

From 7th grade on, nothing in my life or in my world made any kind of sense anymore.

I had such a hard time fitting in anywhere I went.

By the end of my 8th grade year, I lived a pretty lonely and sad existence for a while because all of the friends I grew up with just couldn't understand me anymore and that made me so upset that I would lash out.

I spent so many days and nights wondering what it was all for? Why me? Why was I so different from everyone else? Why can't anyone hear me or see me or understand that I am truly a good person and I have no ill intentions at all?

How come no one can see that I am just a very lost girl trying to figure out where I fit in?

Between the chaos at home that continued, the absence of my Mother, the friends at school giving up on me and dumping me. (Some of them very cruel to me just to fit in with each other. Some even bullied me beyond what I thought I could deal with at the time. Some told lies about me to the others. Some made fun of my clothes and called me names) ... by the time Freshman year of high school was over, I became very angry inside.

I went from being one of the nicest girls in the world; full of wonder and love of life to a mean and angry bully myself.

I had enough of everyone tormenting me and not understanding me... not believing in me! I was all on my own and I knew it.

Although, I had made many new friends and had people all around me all the time. Even though I would have appeared to the untrained eye to be a popular and happy good student; I was dying inside and felt so alone no matter how many people I was surrounded by.

I mean, I had been walking this lonely path that no one else could understand for so long that I vowed to myself that I would always stand up for myself and always have the courage to speak my truth!!

I was a very troubled girl and no matter who didn't like me, I was bound and determined to hate them more.

I was just done with believing in people and love. I hadn't felt loved in years and when they say "As within, so without"; I was a walking and talking example of it.

I was out of patience, out of Faith, and I had completely lost that beautiful magical free spirit that I had carried around with me for the first part of my life. What was the point? Everyone thought I was crazy when I was me anyway!

I got to the point where if someone picked on my I would just take my aggression out on them, no questions asked! I was radiating darkness from having my heart torn out and since I couldn't feel loved, I sure was not going to go out of my way to make anyone else feel loved either!

I did my very best, though to just put on an act like everything was great and I was happy. I spent more time trying to look like I wasn't a walking and talking tornado!

Most days, I wondered if people around me could feel the huge bleeding ulcer seeping and protruding out of my chest that was the broken and torn apart pieces of my heart.

But, no matter how angry or sad or discombobulated I became, The angelic and heavenly beings that I had been seeing and hearing my whole life continued to give me guidance and trying to steer my ship back into the right shore.

I was bound and determined at that time though to shut them out too. Why were they so worried about me and what I was doing? What was it that they exactly wanted from me? Why couldn't they go bug someone else?

The more I tried to ignore the signs and signals and voices and beautiful energy radiating around myself and other people (that only I could seem to see), the more they would be present. The more I would pull negativity into myself, the more they would send me feelings of joy. I did my best to block the joy out!

12
CHAPTER

The Confirmation

AROUND THE SAME time frame, in and amongst all of the chaos and hard times that I was living in, I was at the point in my Catholic C.C.D. (Confraternity of Christian Doctrine) Journey that it was time for me to start thinking about and planning Confirmation.

Now being "Confirmed" a Member of the Catholic Church meant that as a young adult and on into adulthood, I would be choosing to believe in and stand by the views and rules and rites of the Catholic Church.

I spent many nights laying in my bed and wondering how it could be that what I had experienced my entire life up until that point, was not anywhere near what the adults around me in my home, in my community, in my church were telling me.

I mean, they had been teaching me since I was a young child that you could only speak to Jesus through the priest and the church; but I had been seeing and speaking to Jesus since I was born!

They told me that I should fear Jesus and God and if I did not follow the rules of the church, I would not be loved. But, somehow I felt so loved and so cherished by God and Jesus and Heaven… the angels… Saints always! Even when I was not doing things exactly as I should be. I would hear their messages to change my ways and do good in the world… But I was never ever abolished or shunned or made to feel like I wasn't worthy!

In fact, the only times in my young life back then that I ever felt I fit in was when I was amongst my own soul and my angelic Friends.

The only places I felt I fit in were in nature and amongst the animals and plants when I was young!

The adults at church told me that if I didn't "Confess my sins" that I would go to a place called Hell… Where I would burn for all of eternity.

What always confused me too was that they said if you didn't go to church every week then you would go to hell… but my parents only went once in a while; or would go in streaks.

I spent some time as a child believing that my whole family was going to go to Hell!

Then it became a theme it seemed…

They were always condemning people…

If you didn't believe in God, you would go to hell…

If you didn't bow before you sat in the church pew… you would go to hell…

If you didn't kneel down and then stand up and then kneel down and then sit… the very correct way… Hell for you!

During all of my years of C.C.D, we learned more about what was wrong and bad to do then we learned about love and light and being a kind and loving compassionate person; as I always knew Jesus was when he walked the Earth… even as a young child, I knew Jesus !

I mean I felt like I knew him personally… like I walked beside him during his life.

When they told me he never married and never had kids… even as a child I wanted to tell them that wasn't true… I knew so! I didn't know how I knew… it just felt so true to me!

When they talked about the resurrection and all the things that went on with Jesus's Death… I already knew things about all of it. More than what the adults who were teaching me seemed to be aware of! But I guess at the time I just assumed that everyone knew deep inside.

They taught us that angels only appear during the time of the bible… but I knew that was not true either… I mean I saw them all the time. I mean, I would even see angels while I was sitting in church!

I watched people who would sit in church on Sundays… "sin" all week long.

I mean I saw them in church, and everyone thought they were "holy "people in town… but then I would see them in public and watch them be just mean or untrustworthy.

I started to become very confused about all this "Catholic" stuff.

The priest that I grew up with was not a very friendly man and was rumored to be an alcoholic in private.

I watched adults smile to his face and then talk about him when his back was turned.In fact, I heard him say unjust things about people in the church at times too.

As a child, I was terrified of him and never wanted to displease him.

I will never forget this one particular day my parents took us kids to "Confession".

Even though we were never every week type of Catholics; we still had to go to confession when the church said it was appropriate.

Apparently, my parents had been programmed by their parents that you had to confess your sins during certain weeks of the year, so you didn't go to hell.

My parents were strict in their convictions that even though they didn't attend the church often at all, they wanted to teach us kids to be obedient when it came to confession of our sins.

This was during lent and that was taboo at the time to not go every week during lent.

So there I was sitting there in the pew waiting my turn. I knew that I hadn't done anything that I thought was a Sin all week long.

I leaned over to my dad and said "dad... I didn't sin this week! I don't know what to say when I go in there?"

He just gave me that "be quiet" look he had and then leaned over and whispered in my ear "You have to say something. Just say anything so that you can be forgiven for it!"

Now at this point in my life and in that moment, I was super confused. I mean, was he saying make something up?

Was I supposed to go in there and lie? Say I did something even if I didn't?

But then if I did, then wouldn't that then be sinning?

My heart began to race... my chest was pounding with fright and worry; and then all of a sudden, the door opened up and my brother came walking out and sat in the pew.

My dad nudged me and said, "Go ahead!"

I got up and my stomach churned...

I went into the confessional and knelt down... respectfully made the sign of the cross and then said, "Forgive me Father for I have sinned!"

I was panicking. what was I going to say?

He replied, "When was your last confession?"

I said, "It has been 1 week!"

"Well, how have you sinned in the last 7 days?" he asked.

Like word vomit it came out "I was mean to my sister one-day last week!"

He eagerly replied, "Ok, but what are your sins?"

I said, "I don't know. I have been a really good girl and fighting with my sister is the worst thing I have done since my last confession. Will you forgive me Father?"

There was a silence...

He said, "Say the Hail Mary and the Our Father with me and then you will be forgiven."

So, I said the prayers with him, and I left the confessional.

After everyone in our family was done spilling our guts, I thought we were free to go and stood up to leave.

However, the priest came out of the confessional and pulled my dad aside. He asked my dad if he could please speak to him in private.

My intuition kicked into overdrive and I had a strong feeling that the private conversation was about me. I mean, I hoped it wasn't, but I knew the frustration that I felt deep inside of the Priest when he was speaking with me.

After we left, my dad talked to me and said, "Did you tell Father Tom that you were mean to your sister?"

"Yes... You told me to say something... and I didn't know what to say!"

To my surprise, my dad laughed and put his big hand on my shoulders and said, "Well the Priest thought it was funny, because you were telling on yourself!"

Suddenly, the laugh turned into his disappointed look and my dad asked me, "Would you like to please now confess to me, exactly what you did to your sister last week?"

That was when I realized that I had gotten away with taking my new-found anger of life out on my sister; until now!

I then, without reservation, got in trouble then for something I had done a week prior... Punishment and all...

I was so confused... The priest was making a joke out of my confession? The adults think it's cute and funny?

How can adults think it's funny, but be mad at me for it at the same time?

I didn't think it was funny at all... I was mortified... I was embarrassed.

All of this religious confusion that I had been experiencing since I was a small child continued to run through my mind for the next several months.

I eventually reached a point where I had decided that I did not want to be a Catholic.

In fact, I had already made up my mind that I didn't feel truth in being Catholic; not at all!

I had a strong calling within my own spirit, that told me I did not need to listen to what other Human Beings told me "God" was.

Instead, I could almost hear the Heavens telling me, that I should listen to what my own heart and soul said was truth for me.

I just wanted to be a good girl who Loved God for whatever "God" was; which I still wasn't sure of at that point, but I sure wanted to know.

I knew for sure that I wanted to have a strong relationship with the Divine, but without all of the confusion of guilt and shame that Being Catholic seemed to place upon people.

I had always loved and felt truth in Jesus and I somehow just knew that I did not need a church or a religion in order to have my own personal relationship him.

I figured I had always done my very best to be my own sort of disciple of Love and Light.

I mean, until recently, when sadness, shame, and anger had been my main emotions that I carried; even if it was in private.

I had always tried my best to do good in the world.

I was old enough and intelligent enough at that time to know what was best for me and my life.

I knew I had to tell my parents that deep inside my being, I did not believe in the Catholic Church and all of its rules and stories.

But how was I going to do this with Parents who were both born and raised Catholic. How would I find the courage to stand out from the crowd and speak my truth; when both extended families had been filled with people and children who never questioned anything…just willingly conformed? Because it was what everyone had been taught to do; just be confirmed into whatever religion or beliefs that their families had.

Had no one ever questioned this before? Why was I the only one who seemed to feel differently and see it in a different light?

There I was, once again, the black sheep of the family! Both of my older brothers had been confirmed Catholic; neither of them questioned our parent's beliefs…

Oh my, why did I always have to be so different than everyone else? I could back down and just get confirmed, because it would make my parents proud and happy if I did.

I guess I could choose to just be "Normal" and go with the flow for once. But, when I thought of doing it just to make them happy, all I could think of was how miserable I would be; pretending to believe in and follow things that felt so untrue to my heart and soul.

I thought about it over and over and decided that I must choose me, no matter what! I was strongly being called to choose me...

I knew that I had to be true to myself! Even if it meant I would get into trouble or be shunned from the family.

One morning I got up and I decided that it was the day I would speak my truth to my parents.

I sat down with both of them and said, "Please do not be mad at me, but I do not think I want to get confirmed as a Catholic!"

My mom said "Why?"

I took a deep breath and said "Because I just do not believe in it. I feel there is so much more to everything then what they teach.

It doesn't feel like truth to me. I just don't feel like I belong there and when I am an adult, I am definitely not going to take my children to a catholic church as a place of worship!"

After the deep breath was gone and all of that had already spilled out of my mouth like word vomit; I braced myself.

I keenly watched my parents and took note of both of their body languages; which to my surprise were not closed off.

My mom said, "Well when you are an adult it is your choice!"

Within seconds, my dad said, "You do not have to get confirmed then. If it is not what you feel is right for you, then we will support you!"

I could not believe it... I thought for sure I was going to be in big trouble.

At the time, I didn't yet realize how important that conversation would be in my life going forward.

I never went back to C.C.D. again.

Although, I still was expected to attend church and be a part of what my family was doing at church until I was and adult.

I was ok with that… fair enough!

I would take this as a sign that I should always stand up for what I believed in and walk my own path; even if it wasn't a popular path.

I was determined that if I would just continue to be a good person and do right in the world, that I would show them that they were not making a mistake by letting me be me!

I would continue to do good in school and make a good name for myself.

I spent most of the rest of that year alone in my room writing stories and connecting with my new connection with "God"; even though I still couldn't define any of it yet.

I made the decision right then and there to let go of the sadness and anger I had deep inside and just be thankful for what I had.

I may not have felt like I fit in anywhere, but at least I was given permission to be me! That was the greatest gift my parents could have ever given to me at that time (more than they will ever know).

In an effort to be a good student and follow the norms of society; I joined the cheerleading squad and did all I could to try and be "normal".

But it seemed like the better of a girl I was, the more my mom would stop coming home from work and my dad was angry about it all of the time.

My oldest brother wouldn't seem stop doing things to stir up trouble at home; and the fights between him and my dad became physical to the point where he ran away one day and never came back.

I became the punching bag, or so it felt like for everyone around me...

I just couldn't win... I was alone all the time... except for when I would sit out in nature, under a tree or just lay in the grass... Or go into the woods... I would feel loved so completely.

I would see angels and flashes of light when I was in nature.

It was around that time that I saw my first Fairy in the woods... they were always surrounding me back then...

Even though it had felt like the entire world of Humans had turned their backs on me; I had other friends. celestial "Friends" who although I didn't quite understand it... made me feel so loved.

13

CHAPTER

Bad Girls Club

THE CHAOS AND hard times continued at home and my mom was hardly around anymore shortly after that.

Once again it was made apparent to me that no matter how hard things got here on Earth; my real "Friends" were always there with me to keep me going.

I had given up on having any Human friends in my life, because no one seemed to understand me at all anyway.

I just wanted to get through high school and then go far away!

Until one day in the beginning of my Sophomore year, a girl I barely knew sat in front of me in Math class.

She turned around and said "Hey, do you want skip class with me?"

I was mortified at first… like who does this girl really think I am?

The thought crossed my mind in that moment; Is that what people think of me now, that I am a bad and naughty girl who skips class?

But before I could even respond, she repeats herself "Hey. Do you want to skip class with me?"

I replied, "I don't want to get in trouble!"

She laughs and says "You won't get caught, trust me! When the bell rings, just follow me out the door and do not look back, okay?"

I couldn't even answer her before the bell rang and she said, "Here we go!"

My heart was pounding, and I knew that I was going to be in big trouble! We walked out the door and kept walking.

I Didn't look back and it was one of the most empowering things I think I have ever done!

That was the day that I realized I had a choice... I could continue to wallow in my sorrows for friendships lost, parents who didn't understand me, and dreams that never came true;

Or I could embrace the here and now and allow myself to open to a new path!

I stepped onto that new path and let go of the old for the first (of what would end up being many) time in my life; and that girl ended up being one of the very best friends I would ever have to this day she is still near and dear to my heart!

Yes, I was hanging out at Haberman Park (which was a park well known for drugs ad bad kids), and yes I was skipping school (which was a huge no-no if you wanted to make the honor roll); but I found myself for the first time in my entire life surrounded by people who welcomed me and celebrated the person I was.

In the days, weeks, months, and couple of years ahead, I developed some of the best friendships and bonds that I still have today (many of them).

I found out that these weren't horrible Human Beings at all…
They were just as lost as I was!

Many of them in similar home life situations as I was.

We all helped each other feel loved and we all just found peace
and contentment in each other's company.

I finally found a family in that group of "Bad" kids; which
after I stopped judging them and joined them, I realized several
of them were like me.

Many of them saw and heard and felt things that others didn't!

In fact, one of them lived in a broken down old house in Lodi,
where we hung out after school and at night.

Her mom would let us drink and do whatever we wanted to.
None of us really gave a care about much in those days other than
just being together.

We had made our own family!

So, for the next couple of years I became a "Bad girl". In fact,
me and the girls I ran with called ourselves "the Bad Girls Club".

It didn't seem correct for me, as I was a lover by nature… but
life had made me hard and I was not about to be treated like I was
treated freshman year ever again!

I became that girl that people were afraid to cross. I started
physically fighting all the time and I was well known as the girl
that would beat you up bad!

I started to stand up for those kids that were bullied and
kicked around, and I started stepping up for those who were
picked on. I would bully the bullies and I never ever lost a fight;
I became revered… And respected.

Anytime anyone that I cared about had a problem, they would come to me and I would handle it for them; even if that meant I would slam a head into a locker or take someone to the ground and show them what for!

My senior year I was suspended from school for a fight I got into where I hurt the girl severely.

Why did I do it? Because she was picking on my best friend and that was not tolerated back then.

It was a loyalty thing for me. These people I had taken on as my family had shown me loyalty like no one ever had.

I felt like I owed it to them to take care of them. I had an overwhelming need to be needed and be special; even if it meant I would do unthinkable things to those who crossed any of us!

During those days, I tried my best to put a smile on my face and make it look like I was enjoying life.

But, secretly, I was filled with so much anger and resentment for how I had been rejected by others my entire life. The feeling of being shoved aside from my parents was so deep within my being that I would just wait for the right moment to find an excuse to take my aggression out on an unsuspecting person.

I hid my true feelings so deep inside myself and did everything I could to make it look like I was enjoying it when I would take it out on someone who "Deserved it".

The scary part was that by then, I had felt so abandoned and rejected by my own family that I truly didn't care anymore.

What was the point of life? To be born into a family that didn't really want you around?

To be that weird girl that might be on the verge of losing her mind from all of the things she saw and felt? But in the end knew that she could not ever share with another soul (but she hid it so well that no one around her had a clue that she was experiencing any of it)...

I mean, I was on the verge of becoming an adult and to me it was pointless... a life of pure deep-seated excruciating pain from all of the lies that she ended up having to tell to people so that they would have no clue that her home life was as bad as it was.

Rejection so far into my soul that I wasn't sure how to even deal with it or understand it for that matter...

No peace anywhere to be found except when I was with my "Bad" friends who also had messed up home lives and no one to turn to.

So we hung out and got drunk and beat people up to secretly feel like we were successful at something!

At least for me it was. I had never been famous before for anything or known until I earned the name "Rocky" in high school.

14
CHAPTER

The Darkness continues

ALTHOUGH DEEP WITHIN my being, I knew I was not intended for a life of crime or being "bad"; I had such a hard time pulling myself out of the new-found darkness that seemed to take over my life.

At that point in my life, I was having mystical experiences daily. (I see it now, but I didn't then)

There were always angels around me; even though I ignored their pleas to try and steer me back on to my path.

I had unusual experiences with Humans that I would run into in public. They would say profound things to me. I recognized these "people" from my childhood. I knew that they were not Human and that the experiences were not happening by accident.

Everything about my intuition continued to tell me that I was a bit off the path, but could easily reel it in and get back on track if I was willing!

I ignored what my intuition was saying to me. Why should I listen? I listened when I was a little girl and it did nothing but get me made fun of, laughed at, and called a liar.

So truly what is the point of any of this. Might as well just be bad; at least I am good at something for the first time in my life, besides swimming, singing, and writing, which I excelled in at school.

Most of my senior year of high school was spent skipping school, getting drunk, and being a bully.

Why? Because I just gave up on life and didn't care anymore.

15
CHAPTER

A second chance at love

THEN ONE DAY, I left home... I just packed my things that decided there was no point in being there anymore!

My Mother was never there when I was, and my dad was always angry and I just couldn't take it any longer!

I lived in my car for about a week and then one day in town, I ran into my sister Tammy.

In spite of us living in the same town, I hadn't seen her in over a year.

She told me she had recently gone through a divorce and that if I needed a place to stay, I was welcome to stay with her and babysit her children for her in return.

For the first time in a long time, I felt like I had a chance to get back on track and have a family to belong to!

Yes! This was meant to be, I could feel it! I would live with my sister and her and I would be family!!! I would love her children like they were my own!

Maybe this is the breakthrough I had been looking for!

It started out to be more than amazing! It was more than I could have ever imagined it would be. Tammy and I were working together as partners keeping the house clean and taking care of the kids.

I can honestly say, it was going really well! Her and I were finally getting to know each other.

Our connection was out of this world and I was amazed at how much we were alike, even though we never grew up together… it was like we were twins (except she was 9 years older).

She had angels all around her home too! She had a spirit that was just as bright as mine… but I wasn't sure if I could tell her… did she know?

I saw many spirits in and out of her home all of the time and she never seemed to notice them… So I never said anything.

I absolutely loved living with her… the light in me shined so brightly when I was with her.

But I was in what would be one of the darkest times of my life thus far and I just couldn't seem to get things right… no matter how hard I tried to only do good!

At that time in my life, darkness followed me… it was like I was cursed…

Everywhere I went bad things would happen!

No matter how hard I tried to make the best thing in my life last, my friends would come over and steal from my sister.

I knew for sure that I had nothing to do with the shenanigans. I would never do that to her; I had too much love and respect for her.

But it didn't seem to matter; the people who I called my friends were in the place that I was before I moved in with Tammy. They were lost and broken and simply didn't care.

All I knew for sure was that I never wanted to lose my sister, as she was the only one in the world who seemed to understand me!

Unfortunately, it didn't take long for the magic of the love between two sisters to be interrupted by the darkness that surrounded me!

Just like everything else that was ever good in my life; my relationship with her would go out in flames too one night when I decided to have a couple people over who I thought were friends!

Just like you see in the movies, they invited a few people... who invited a few people... you know the story!

As if it wasn't bad enough that an out of control party went on and my best friend broke her arm on my sister's property that night!

The worst part was that her arm was broken by the guy I had a huge crush on; who threw her down to the ground out on the sidewalk.

Tammy was nearly sued by my friend's mother.

Much to my dismay, the people who I thought were my "Friends "had also stolen expensive jewelry out of my sister's bedroom that night.

Mainly a diamond ring that was given to her handicapped son when he was a baby.

Although I truly and honestly didn't know who the thief was; I had to take the blame for it, since I allowed those people into her home.

Much to my surprise, she loved me enough to forgive me.

However, she made me promise I would never let any friends come into her home again if I was going to continue to live with her.

Due to my age, my attitude, and the way I felt about myself, I disrespected her and had my friend over one day... just for a few minutes... just quickly to grab something...

Tammy came home unexpectedly and caught us... kicked me out and I was once again homeless.

I could have cared less about not having somewhere to stay. what hurt me the most was that I indirectly hurt her.

The one who held her arm out and held my hand when no one else cared!

By this time, I saw it clearly finally. I just knew I was a bad person. No wonder why my Mother didn't want to come home.

I mean, no wonder why everyone around me kept leaving my life!

I finally realized how awful I was.

Even when I was trying to be a good person... bad things happened and even if it wasn't my fault, it always seemed to appear that way... so I must be the one causing it all.

With the new-found knowledge I had about myself, I figured I should make it up to my Parents.

I mean, I truly believed that I was probably the reason that my mom wasn't coming home.

I must have been a very bad person... I felt sorry for those who had to be around me.

No wonder my biological Father left me when I was a baby.

I apologized to my parents for leaving and then I went back home to the farm for a very short time after that.

I got my own apartment because things at home just would not calm down it seemed and since no one was aware of how lost and broken I was, why would I stay there?

I had been the one apologizing my whole life so far; but I couldn't be the only one who was trying to make things right.

I just didn't fit in anywhere, expect amongst those who were lost and broken too.

16
CHAPTER

Is it just my imagination?

ONE NIGHT ABOUT a month after moving into my own apartment I decided to have a party.

How awesome this would be? A bunch of teenage kids, no parents and lots of alcohol.

We would have to much fun and no limits, right?

Besides, the way I saw it that night was; if it wasn't too much fun, then maybe I could drink myself to death and no one would have to deal with what an awful person I was.

I figured, either way, everyone wins!!!!

I was done being good and I just wanted the beings around me to leave me alone! Stop following me! Stop trying to make me be good! I didn't care anymore!

Maybe I deserved to go to hell (I thought) …

As I gathered all of the supplies that I would need to host an epic drinking party and also be the life of said epic party; I went down to the local liquor store where they thought I was 21 and never carded me!

I walked back to the cooler and much to my surprise I saw a man standing there that looked like Jesus.

He was holding the cooler door open and the light from the cooler was very bright.

My heart pounded because I suddenly remembered all the times when I was a kid and Jesus would walk beside me and talk with me and come into my dreams.

I hadn't connected with him or anything "good" in a very long time and I sure wasn't looking to connect in that moment.

I just wanted him to go away! Leave me alone in my misery and let me be bad!

So I walked back there and with all of my might I stared at the floor hoping that maybe he would go away if I didn't look at him.

I also had the thought just then that maybe it was just my imagination getting the best of me like everyone had been telling me all these years.

Maybe the guilt I felt inside for lying and buying beer at 17 was just getting the best of me. No matter how hard I ever tried to not care, I always had this voice deep inside of me that would not allow me to lie and cheat and steal.

After further review, I figured, I was definitely just making this up because I felt guilty for being in a liquor store.

Jesus was definitely not around me and even if he was, I sure wasn't going to look at him.

I continued to stare at the floor and walked up to the cooler door. Of course, the one I was looking for with the Corona in it was right next to this man who looked like Jesus with the bright light shining all around him.

I opened the cooler door and as fast as I could I grabbed the Corona and slammed that door shut and tried to practically run to the front without making eye contact.

As soon as I started my journey back up the aisle, I heard "Well Hello There!"

'UUUGH" I thought to myself and took a few more steps away and I thought I could ignore it.

I tried to ignore the voice. I continued to stare at the floor.

I heard "What do you think of all the Minors who have been getting caught intoxicated lately?"

I think about every swear word I knew went through my head and I awkwardly said, "I haven't heard!"

I looked down to the floor again and started to walk ever so slightly faster, almost tripping over my own two feet.

He said "Really? Yeah, they are drinking much younger these days than they used to. It's quite a shame because the parents aren't really around anymore, and kids really do not know their limits and they can endanger themselves from drinking too much!"

I stopped dead in my tracks and turned around just for a split second; because I just couldn't believe that he seemed to know about my secret thoughts I had earlier (you know the ones where I thought about drinking myself to death).

I mean, why won't he stop following me around? Why won't he just let me be bad? I wondered if I was seriously losing my mind finally?

I looked straight at him one more time... I just needed to see this man one more time to see if I was losing my mind... Was I losing my mind?

I saw him smile and say, "Please be careful and heed my warning" and then I slowly saw him vanish.

Now, because everyone had always told me I was imagining it, I assumed that this time was no different and I of course ignored what was said; for the most part.

However, I could not get it out of my head for weeks; of course, never shared it with anyone until now.

About a month later I drank so much Corona one night that I was throwing up blood and was sick on the couch for days. And like clockwork the whole scenario came to my head and I asked myself if that was the warning he was trying to give; but then I brushed it off as nonsense, since I was just imagining it. Coincidence? Or just a freak thing... yeah just a freak thing; I wasn't gonna let some dude tell me what to do anyway!

17

CHAPTER

The Journey

A COUPLE OF weeks later I went to a party in a very bad neighborhood in Madison.

I was told that it was a "Journey" party and that anyone who went there was gonna go on a Journey.

I was excited, because I never did any sort of "Journey" before, but I sure thought it would be amazing!

I had no idea what I was in for. We walked into the doorway and up a steep set of stairs to a very shady looking apartment.

Every single room held different drugs and a different theme. Depending on what you wanted to experience you could do one or all of the rooms.

I was so scared! Not because of what was going on in there, but because of what I could see in the rooms that no one else seemed to be aware of.

That was the first time in my life that I truly thought I was losing it. I watched as some very scary entities where hovering up above and all around the people who were smoking crack in one room.

In the next room there was a different set of dark entities giggling and laughing at the people who were doing heroin.

It was like they were feeding off of the people's energy (but at the time I had never heard of such a thing). I saw it with my own eyes though!

I couldn't bear to look in any other rooms. I had enough and just wanted to get out of there!

The next thing I knew, the people I was with gave me a little piece of paper and told me to put it on my tongue.

"What is this?" I asked.

"That is how you Trip Balls" someone said, and they all laughed.

"Don't you want to go on a journey with us?" Another guy asked.

"Come on chicken... just do it! You will see beautiful trails and colors. It's nothing bad, just open your mind!" I heard coming from a tall and skinny stranger who smiled like the Cheshire Cat on Alice in Wonderland.

"What is it though?" I asked

Suddenly, one of my guy friends said. "That my love is Acid. Strychnine... The golden ticket to the most magical journey of your lifetime!"

As fast as I could try to say no thank you, I will have a beer; he quickly shoved it in my mouth and said "Relax, you are with us, you will be fine!"

"Ok... I said. I trust you!"

Little did I know at the time that it would certainly be one of the most "Magical" journeys of my lifetime up until that point; but not in the way that he meant it (I don't think anyway).

I do not have a whole lot of recollection of that night except for the "Journey" I went on which I do believe was the first time I truly had a near death experience.

I know I was out of my body and I know for sure that I was not making it up for the first time in my life. I saw all of what Heaven is and I saw everything so very clearly!

You can try to convince me that it was just an "Acid trip", but I know what I experienced, what I saw, and where I went. At least my consciousness did, I know for sure!

I walked down a street which looked exactly like the yellow brick road that I saw as a kid when I watched Wizard of oz.

Truthfully, whoever wrote that must have been on an acid trip very similar to mine. Because a lot of what I saw in Heaven that day looked so much like everything in that movie.

I even saw what appeared to be a huge Golden Gate loaded with Diamonds and surrounded with angels.

The crazy thing is I saw things in that journey that I didn't even realize what they were until years later.

As soon as I was aware enough to be able to move. Now, when I say move, I mean that I was floating around. It was the strangest feeling I had ever felt.

But, when I was aware enough, I was escorted down this "Yellow brick Road" by Jesus himself and as I walked side by side with him.

He said, "I am so happy you are here, but you need to go back soon!"

I felt so amazing being there that I was almost offended by him trying to hurry me along. I mean, I had nothing good going for me back there, why can't I just stay, I thought.

I looked at him and said "Can I please just stay here with you? It feels so much like home here and I have never felt at home before. Please? I will be good and do whatever you want me to do… can I stay?"

He lovingly kept walking beside me and reached out to grab my hand. I graciously accepted the hand holding and we kept walking.

"Beloved… you must go back. You have many big things that are undone yet."

"Why am I here then?" I said, as I felt frustrated. I mean somehow, I knew I was in Heaven or some sort of heavenly realm; so why the heck am I here if I can't stay?"

He smiled and said "You are not listening to my advice! We needed to have a little meeting here, so you would believe that you are not imagining this! This is very real, and I am very real and so are you and your beautiful soul!"

I stood there, confused… "What?" I said.

"Dear one… Some day you will understand all of this. But I want you to trust that everything you have experienced on Earth is truly real. Heaven, Earth, all of existence is counting on you to make the right decisions and to let go of all of that anger you feel deep inside!"

He looked me dead and the eye and continued…

"Listen… You chose this path and you are only a little bit off course. Soon your whole life will change, and you will need to stop getting intoxicated until you black out. It will not help you release the hurt you feel… you know!"

I truly didn't really understand much of what he was saying to me and I just wanted to try to understand... why couldn't I understand? Who am I? What am I supposed to do? Am I alive? Am I dead?

I mean everything, and anything went through my head and my thoughts at that moment.

I replied" How is my life going to change?"

"You will see. In time, you will understand all of this and you will be able to see the path that has been laid before you by those who walked it first. For now, please... Will you -please heed my warning and stop hurting your divine temple like you have been. You have so much coming into your life and it is going to change very soon. I wish I could tell you more, but you won't understand. Just follow my guidance and remember that every path will lead you to the light if you only choose for it to!"

In that moment I felt so angry and so lost! Just broken!

But at the same time, somewhere in all my being I knew that I must heed the warning and that I needed to straighten up!

Shortly after that, I woke up on the floor in a pile of vomit and sat up to see where I was.

I looked around me as I laid there and saw that everyone else who was there was asleep too; I am talking bodies all over the place.

Unfortunately, the people I had come to the party with were nowhere to be found when I walked from room to room.

Then I figured I had better get out of there too since I didn't know anyone there.

As I walked down the steps and out the door, I realized it was daylight. Oh my!!!… It was morning!

I walked out to my car and started it up and sat there for what seemed like a long time… just trying to figure it all out.

I drove home and all I knew was that I would never ever be the same again… and I would never ever doubt the validity of what I saw and heard and felt.

How could any of that be imagined, I thought? Well, or maybe I am just losing my mind here?

I went home and couldn't shake the experience; but also couldn't share it with anyone. People would never speak to me again if I shared that story.

Either way, no one would believe me!

I stopped drinking to dangerous levels, and I started attending school again immediately after that; because although I didn't know why at the time, I just had an overwhelming feeling that I needed to get myself together and graduate high school.

18
CHAPTER

White Buffalo

ABOUT A MONTH later, I had my first lucid dream where a very large Native American Man walked me down a path and showed me a teepee where a woman had just had a baby girl.

The baby was very bright and shiny and had what looked kind of like sparkles and bubbles all around her.

Laying right next to the momma and baby was what looked like a baby white buffalo. Although I had never seen or heard of a white buffalo in my entire life at that time; somehow, I just knew that was what it was.

I awoke the next morning with such a renewed spirit. I felt like I could take on the world. I felt like I had a calling to better the world. An unexplainable new spark was within and all around me.

The only thing was that although I woke up feeling so full of life like never before; I also woke up feeling nauseous.

That weekend I went to Chicago on a girl's trip with one of my best friends at the time. We road tripped and had so much fun.

The only thing that truly stands out to me about the trip though was the fact that no matter what I did, I couldn't keep any food down. I kept vomiting.

It seemed as though, ever since I had that dream about the White Buffalo, I woke up nauseous every single morning.

I kept a package of saltine crackers by my bedside, so that I could settle my stomach before school each morning. It was the strangest thing.

The trip to Chicago was no exception as I somehow knew to bring plenty of Saltines with me!

The people I was in Chicago with were teasing me that I was pregnant. However, I laughed along with them because although I did have a boyfriend at the time (my first love) and we shared the apartment; he worked 3rd shift and we rarely saw each other.

There was no way I could possibly be pregnant. besides, I was on birth control pills and never ever missed one.

On the way home that weekend, we stopped at Burger King and I ordered a chicken sandwich. Back in those days, it was always my favorite choice.

But this particular time, after one whiff and a single bite of the Chicken Sandwich, I had to run to the bathroom and throw up just from smelling it.

As I cleaned myself up after power puking in that Burger King bathroom in Illinois; for the first time ever, I truly just thought to myself... What if I am pregnant? Could it be? I have a month left of high school and then I will be graduated!"

I cleared my head and decided that it couldn't be; I was letting my imagination get the best of me again!

After I dropped everyone off from our road trip, I secretly stopped at the drug store and bought a pregnancy test! My mind was just racing!

I decided that I would take the test the following morning, since then it would be Monday.

I didn't get a whole lot of sleep that night; I was freaking out! This was not what I had planned, and I thought, "What if I truly was pregnant?"

Suddenly, I had the overwhelming feeling of that lucid dream about the Native American mommy and baby and white buffalo overcome me. I felt as though I was instantly transported to that dream again.

I could feel the feeling of having life within my physical body. I could sense that there was something different about my energy.

When I pulled myself back into physical reality, I could not help but wonder; "Is that what that dream was about?"

Then my logical mind stepped in and told that that it can't be.

The thoughts went through my head over and over and over again!

I woke up the next morning and went to the bathroom and took the test. Within a few seconds 2 very distinct pink lines appeared; just as it said on the box would happen if it was a positive result!

I was completely thrown back physically, emotionally, mentally. In every single way possible!

The only thing that was truly swirling through my mind was the liquor store experience, the out of body experience, and the lucid dream I had.

I sat there just completely motionless! Everything and anything going through my mind.

I looked up the number for planned parenthood in the phone book (we didn't have internet or cell phones back then, we had phonebooks and land lines).

I called planned parenthood and they told me to come in right away when they opened at 8am.

I went to the bedroom and knelt down in prayer as my grandmother had shown me to do as a small child. I figured this would be the perfect time to get back to basics of building my relationship again with "God" (whatever that was).

I prayed for direction; because I knew that I had a huge duty here before me. I knew that I needed to completely turn my life around so that I could take this left turn on my journey.

I called out loud "Jesus, where are you? Are you listening to me? I need to see you! Please, I need to talk to you. I promise you, I will listen. I will be good! God please help me… Please God… Help me!"

But nothing happened; for the first time in my life, I felt like I was on my own! I didn't have any visions, I couldn't see any signs! I didn't feel any sort of presence around me!

Except for the spirit of a child that was inside of me. And honestly, even before I went to planned parenthood to confirm my findings, I already could feel this beautiful baby girl inside of me!

I knew with everything I was that I was going to have a beautiful baby girl! How I knew, I have no clue; but with all my being I just felt it! I just knew!

As soon as Planned Parenthood opened that morning, I went and had the tests done. Of course, as I knew they would, the tests confirmed that I was with child.

On my way home from there, I saw pink everywhere. I saw a semi-truck with a cradle on the side that said Haley's Comet on it.

I knew right then and there that I would have a daughter and I would name her after that famous Comet (spelled a tad different than the comet though because I was unique and wanted my child's name to be too.)

19
CHAPTER

The Magna Carta

AFTER THAT DAY, I completely turned my life around. I stopped skipping school and buckled down like never before. I was focused and had a great reason to get right with the universe.

I eventually, got myself on the right path and started planning for the life of raising a child.

When I was pregnant, I could have cared less about anything else in the whole entire world except for my baby!

For the first time in my life, I would love and be loved unconditionally! I was so excited that I would be able to make the right choices for my baby. I vowed within the first month of my pregnancy that I would never ever allow her to go through the things I had to go through as a child. I promised myself and my unborn baby that I would never ever let her or any other child under my wings feel unloved like I did!

Come Hell or high water, I was determined to do better than my parents did. I knew it wasn't going to be easy, but I was up for the challenge and couldn't wait to see how this new chapter in my storybook of life would go!

I was ecstatic that after everything I had been through in my short 18 years of life, I would finally have a family!

It was the strangest thing though… while I was pregnant with my beautiful daughter, I saw the words white buffalo everywhere I went it seemed. I would see buffalo everywhere too!

I couldn't get the vision out of my head that I had seen when I was at the "Journey" party of a white buffalo. I just knew it had to mean something!

I also became very connected to Heaven when she was within me! It was almost like I was a wide-open channel between Heaven and Earth. More than ever before, I could see, hear, sense, and know things that I wasn't sure what to do with.

Not to mention that suddenly, my angelic friends started coming into my bedroom at night again (that hadn't happened in many years).

I just knew without knowing that this child was going to be very special. I would have dreams of her saving lives when I was pregnant with her too. I never knew why but I Just had a strong feeling that she would be a very special child and I was honored to be her mom.

About 3 weeks before she was born, I had a dream that I was standing in a field of wild flowers and a large shiny iridescent angel stood before me.

I asked, "Why are you here?"

The Angel lovingly smiled at me at said "Beloved Child… you know not what you behold, do you?"

I had no clue what that meant, and so I said, "I am very thankful for you and I am happy you are here; but I do not know what I behold, you are right!"

The Angel took my hand and said "one, two, one, five... Some day you will understand. You and your child are very special beings"

Just as I tried to say something back; I watched as she/he seemed to disappear through an invisible door.

I was so confused, and I had no idea what that even meant. How could it be that I was visited by such a beautiful angel. I mean, I will never forget the shimmer I saw in my dream that night. It appeared like a silvery white fire; Radiating like the sun.

When I woke up the next day, I went to the library to try and find out what my dream meant.

At the time, there was not internet... just the Library and books about dreams and angels.

I must have read about 30 books that day trying to figure it all out. I just knew that there was a profound message in that dream.

But truly the only thing I really learned was that the angel I saw in my dream that night was most likely Archangel Gabriel.

I felt it as truth, so deep inside when I saw a picture that someone else drew of what they had witnessed. I was amazed when the picture I saw of Archangel Gabriel was almost identical to what I saw in the dream.

All I could really get from it was that Maybe Gabriel would be my child's "Guardian" angel?

And at that time, all I knew was that 1-2-1-5 had absolutely no meaning. So I let it go for the time being.

What I didn't know at the time was that I would end up giving birth to my only daughter on December 15, 1993 (even though I wasn't due until December 20th).

I must mention quickly here that she came 5 days early. Not to mention the fact that her Birth Day was the 15th, which is 5 x 3.

Remember in the beginning of the book when I said that I am surrounded in the energy of 5? So this takes my birth a little deeper into the realms of change and transformation!

I didn't figure it out until years later that 1-2-1-5 would end up being my daughter's date of birth. I knew it had to be something significant; not just any old birth; because why would I dream that?

I later found out through signs and synchronicities I saw in a book published around 2003; that 1215 was the "Year of the Magna Carta" which had something to do with the struggles of Woman and Children in medieval England and a woman who stood up for the rights of herself and her beautiful child (who she viewed as a diamond or Jewel).

I almost fainted when I saw this book at a book store one day when my daughter was about 10 years old.

it aligned with all the synchronicities that I saw when I was pregnant with my daughter. To this day, I have never shared any of it with anyone until now.

I have a strong feeling that my daughter and I were probably there and had a hand in the "Magna Carta" ... But of course, that is just a hunch!

It also talked about how students back in that time were strongly encouraged to study in the Medical field... (my daughter and I now a days are both very educated in the medical field in so many ways... it's like second nature to us...)

It truly makes me believe in all of us being here on Earth many times... and for very specific purposes.

20
CHAPTER

Life's Little Surprises

AS IF IT wasn't synchronistic enough with everything I saw and heard and learned about my daughter's spirit; things were just as magical when I got pregnant with my biological son in August of 1994.

You see, when I got pregnant with my daughter, I was on the birth control pill and I never missed a dose.

So, when I got pregnant once while on birth control, I chalked it up to "Must have been meant to be".

But, after I gave birth to my daughter; at my 6-week checkup post birth…I had what was called "Norplant" surgically placed in my upper arm.

This was to prevent pregnancy for around 5 years. I knew I wasn't quite ready to have another child and that I wouldn't be ready for quite some time.

I had growing up to do for one thing; and for another, I truly wanted to finish college before I even thought about another bun in the oven.

Not to mention that things were not that great between my daughter's father and I (We were high school sweethearts and each other's firsts…We had clearly outgrown each other by a long shot but wanted to try and make it work for the sake of our beautiful daughter.)

We eventually went our separate ways in spring of 1994, and it wasn't very long until I started to date another man.

I will be very honest; with the lack of self-love and self-identity I still struggled with beneath the surface, at that age I thought I had to be with someone. It didn't really matter at what cost, as long as I had someone to be co-dependent on.

After my new love and I were together for about a month, I had another angel dream.

This time the angel was a fiery green color and wings were translucent.

I will never forget the dream, because the angel appeared to me at the end of my bed one night and said, "A child will heal your heart in ways you never thought possible."

This time I did not want to lose connection with the angel before I got solid answers on why he/she was here and what the message was!

I cried out "What is it that you want from me? Why are you here?"

Just then, I heard a distinct voice say "You are being prepared for a sacred Journey of the heart. A sort of initiation. You will need true and real Faith to pass this test!"

"What test?" I exclaimed…

"Is this just a dream?" I asked out of desperation.

The angel said "Please never underestimate the power of Heaven and Earth. Never give up on the impossible" …

I was frustrated, because I needed more... I wanted more... I longed for straight answers this time.

I assumed that the dream was about my daughter again and I asked, "Can you please tell me what you know about my daughter?"

I watched, once again, as the angel seemed to escape through what appeared to be an invisible doorway or curtain.

When I woke up the next day, I wanted so badly to talk to someone about what I had experienced.

Honestly though, back then, there wasn't a single soul in my life that would even come close to believing me and I did not want my new love to think I jumped on the crazy train!

I kept it all in and kept it quiet. I just took notes as I continued to have dream after dream where I was climbing up a tall brick wall. Every time I would climb, just as I got too tired to keep going, something would pick me up and safely and smoothly drop me off on the other side of the wall. (I had this dream repeatedly for 2 weeks).

The following week I had Knee Surgery scheduled. I was about to have some clean up done on an old tee-ball injury from childhood.

I went to bed on the night before surgery and suddenly had an overwhelming feeling like I was "with child".

I couldn't shake the feeling, even though I had a 5-year contraceptive placed in my arm. I had only been seeing my new Man for about 2 months, so I felt ashamed to even have the thoughts at first.

It was an "all of a sudden" type of thing. I couldn't shake it. I couldn't sleep. I laid there wide awake all by myself wondering suddenly if those dreams, I had about the green Angel were about a new child that was growing in my womb?

I thought to myself "that's impossible!"

I paused… remembered the dream once again. Suddenly, like a streak of lightening, I felt such a strong urge to get out of bed and drive to the drug store to get a pregnancy test.

I didn't want to wake my sleeping New Boyfriend, so I figured I would take the test in the morning when I got up to scrub up my leg for surgery (back then you would scrub your leg with Iodine at home before you went to the hospital for surgery… standard procedure at that time).

I don't think I slept a wink that night, because once again, my "Friends" were in my room (I hadn't seen them since I had given birth to my daughter).

Before I took the test, I just knew that I was pregnant with a little boy.

The next morning, I got up, took the test with the first morning's urine as recommended and then proceeded to scrub up my leg for surgery.

After I was done scrubbing, I looked at the test and it had a very faint 2nd pink line (1 line = not pregnant… 2 lines = pregnant) so I called the hospital and said "Hello? Um… I don't know how to say this but; I think I need to cancel surgery today!"

The Surgical Nurse said, "Mind if I ask why?"

I replied "well… I have a very faint 2nd pink line on a pregnancy test this morning; even though I have Norplant in my arm!"

"Oh… yeah you better call your primary doctor and go see her immediately!" the Nurse advised.

"But for now, we will cancel knee surgery, as it is not worth losing a baby over if you are pregnant!"

I ended up going in to see my Doctor within a couple hours and the test there showed positive too; but very faint.

She told me to act like I was pregnant and come back in 2 weeks. She said, "It's very early."
She removed the Norplant from my arm right away that day and I went home to tell the miraculous news to my family.

"How could this be?" I thought all the way home.
I was in such shock. This was the 2nd time I got pregnant when I wasn't supposed to. I must really be meant to have this child too I thought.
I couldn't stop thinking of the dreams with the wall climbing and the thoughts and symbolisms of getting easily carried over obstacles after doing the hard work.

Funny thing was that at the time I thought it was because of having 2 babies. I figured that's what the dreams meant.
I assumed that the Angel in the dream was trying to prepare me in advance for the challenges of having a 2nd child so young.
I already figured it would be hard to work, go to school, and have 2 babies. But I was tough, and I could handle anything if I just kept moving forward! I would be helped by my angels.

Little did I know how wrong I would be! The entire pregnancy with my 2nd child was a huge challenge.
If it wasn't one thing one day, then it was another or a few other things on another day!
I started to feel this child moving around inside of me much earlier than I did with my daughter.

I watched for signs a lot more, because just like the first time, I felt a wide-open channel running through me when I was pregnant with my son. I saw angels everywhere during my pregnancy. I felt so much love radiating from my pregnant belly. I knew that whoever this little being was inside of me, he/she must be pretty special!

21
CHAPTER

Secrets of an upstairs apt

I HAD SOME extremely profound experiences when I was pregnant with each of my children. The one I recall the most was when I was about 6 months along with my son.

We had just moved into a new apartment and the first night we slept there I had a vision (or was it a dream?) that I gave birth to a baby angel.

The baby angel had wings. The most gorgeous rainbow-colored wings that were invisible to everyone else except me and this child!

When I woke up the next day, I felt surrounded by Heaven once again.

But soon after moving into the new apartment it didn't feel so heavenly anymore.

It was an upstairs apartment and it was the first time since before I got pregnant with my daughter that I felt "Darkness" around me.

I cannot explain it, but that apartment had very bad "energy".

I would see very dark and evil spirits around me when I was trying to sleep.

I was very scared at first, but I also knew that I must be brave. I knew I couldn't share any of it with my boyfriend, as he didn't know any of my secrets.

I felt like I should share at times, because I would see them all around him. I would see a shadow figure that followed him around and It would seem to make him say and do nasty things.

At times I couldn't believe it and I thought once again, maybe I was just imagining it.

It was a very challenging time of my life, as I had a young baby girl and a child inside of me and I started to feel like I was in my own world again.

My boyfriend at the time loved to go out without me to the bars and his best friend was a known cheater. I heard many stories of him cheating on me while I was pregnant and sitting home.

Although I knew the stories were true, I didn't want to be a failure once again, so I stayed and tried to make it work. One night I had the stomach flu very bad and was very worried about being dehydrated and pregnant.

I asked him to please take me to the hospital and he told me that he had to go to a funeral of his ex-girlfriend's father who had passed away.
He left me at the side of the toilet vomiting and never returned until the next day. I ended up in the Emergency Room and he could have cared less.

I heard a few days later that he spent the night with a girl we both knew; and yes they slept together (he denied it... But I knew better).

I figured that must have been my karma; since when I first started seeing him, he had a girlfriend that he dumped to be with me (since I was the only girl for him... or so he told me in the beginning... until I got pregnant and he got bored).

I spent most of my pregnancy alone with my daughter and my unborn child growing inside of me.

The darkness had returned once again and once again my quest to find a "family" had failed.

I was truly starting to think that maybe I wasn't meant to have a "Family"

22
CHAPTER

My Miracle Baby

SO, I JUST got by day to day and then one morning when I was 7 months along, I woke up soaking wet.

I got up and changed my clothes and laid back down... woke up soaking wet again about an hour later.

I knew after about 4 times of the routine, that I wasn't peeing myself and something must be going on.

I woke my boyfriend up and told him I think something is wrong.

I went into the hospital and they confirmed that my water had broken.

"But I am only 7 months along!" I exclaimed.

The doctor came in and said "We will give the baby steroids to develop the lungs just in case we have to deliver. In the meantime, we will try to stop the labor and you will need to lay on your back until its time."

"Did I hear you correct? You want me to lay on my back for 2 months" I asked.

"Yes, until you are due!" she said.

"How could this be?" I thought as I whispered to myself...you cannot lose this baby!

Eventually, they admitted me; they took me to a room, and I laid on my back for about a week.

One morning, I fell asleep... while I slept, I went out of my body once again.

I saw the yellow brick road and I recognized the castles and waited for my Jesus to greet me as he usually did when I went outside of my Human body,

I walked the Yellow brick road... I kept walking. I waited and waited... and waited...

I figured I must keep going.

I wondered where my "Friends" were. Why weren't they there to greet me? What was going on?

I kept walking and all of a sudden, I saw a little boy up ahead.

I walked towards him and I said "Hi there? What is your name?"

As soon as he turned around, I saw his rainbow-colored wings... I couldn't believe it!

"You!!" I said.

"You are the angel Baby from my dreams?"

He smiled at me and took my hand and walked with me down the path.

He led me to what looked like a temple and I sat down and suddenly out of the corner of my eye I saw a bright shining light... it shimmered and shined and flashed with radiance.

When from out of nowhere, I heard a voice say "Beloved... The path is long and sometimes you must walk alone. You must continue to walk it. Someday it will all make sense. If you lose those you love they still walk beside you in Heaven."

I cried out "God? Is that you God? Are you there?"

But I heard nothing more…

In desperation, I screamed out "God… Please help me understand? Is my baby ok?"

Next thing I knew I woke up and was in a hospital bed covered in sweat and surrounded by nurses and doctors who said they almost lost me.

Before I could even understand what had happened, they had me hooked up to machines and I. V's coming out of me everywhere.

A woman doctor walked in and said "Honey, we can't wait any longer. Your placenta has become infected and you and the baby are at huge risk. We have to induce labor!"

I asked, "Will my baby be ok?"

She said "We can't make any promises, but as of right now, the baby is doing much better then you. Please call your family members; if you can't then we can do it for you. You are having this baby immediately!"

I asked "Did something happen to me? I don't remember much?"

"Don't worry about anything, we will do our very best to save you and the baby both!" she said.

"I don't understand… What is wrong with me?" I asked.

The doctor walked out of the room in a hurry after that.

A male nurse in the room said "Hun, you almost died here a few minutes ago. You were talking with me about breakfast and then you suddenly went unconscious.

Your heart stopped beating and you stopped breathing… we brought you back!"

"Why though?" I asked with frustration.

"What is going on?"

The nurse looked at me and said "There are test results that came back this morning showing you have a very bad infection in your blood that was caused by your water breaking. The fluids have become toxic and we need to get that baby out to save both of you!

Also, you are positive for strep, which is extremely dangerous for you and the baby both."

"Oh my God!" I said...

I broke down and cried... how could this be? I know I talked about dying when I was 17, but I didn't mean it, I didn't truly want to die... not anymore... Even though things weren't perfect... at least I had babies who I could love!

I could NOT lose this baby at all costs!

I called my boyfriend and both of our Mothers and they all got there extremely fast.

Within a few minutes of my child's father walking in the door, the sonogram technician came into the room with the machine to see if the baby's head was down enough to deliver naturally.

He said, "As long as you are going to have this baby today, do you want to know if it is a girl or boy?"

"Yes!" we both (The Baby's father and I) said in sync.

I was adamant I didn't want to know until the baby was born and I did the same thing when I had my daughter.

But in these circumstances, I wanted to know... Just in case me or the baby didn't make it through this!

It was then confirmed... It is a Boy!

I already knew that the whole time, but the Human part of us always likes confirmation!

They induced me and within 12 hours I gave birth to a 2 Lb. 2 oz. baby boy.

I gave birth… he didn't cry… in fact, he didn't make a sound!

In what seemed like a repeat of the morning's events; all of a sudden there were tons of people in the room.

I heard someone say "He isn't breathing!"

Within a few moments like a whirlwind they were all gone. My baby was gone too!

I spent the next 8 hours not knowing anything! Was he alive, was he dead? Was he ok?

Then rather abruptly, a nurse came in my room with a wheelchair and said, "Do you want to go see your baby?"

I said "Get that wheelchair out of my way… I will walk!"

I had been through all of that and I still had the strength of an ox it seemed.

They told me I should have been dead. I laughed and said, "It will take a whole lot more than a little infection to kill this girl!"

Little did I know until 6 weeks later; that I had the beginning stages of Cervical Cancer and that was the reason why my water broke.

I ended up being treated and beat that Cancer like it was a drum!

But anyway…

I will never forget the moment I walked into the NICU and saw my son for the very first time.

He didn't have cartilage in his ears yet and his rear end wasn't fully formed. I could barely see his face because it was covered by wires and tubes and IV's coming out of the sides of his head.

They had shaved his hair off and the only thing I could truly see was his soul… his spirit… his beautiful blue energy that I saw radiating out of the sides of his little body.

I knew no one else could see it, so I didn't say anything; but I just knew without knowing that he was the angel baby I had been seeing!

He had the same eyes and cute little nose!

23

CHAPTER

The Last Rites

FROM THE DAY my biological son was born, life once again got very challenging.

My baby boy spent the first 5 years of his life in and out of the hospital... Due to his lungs not being fully developed when he was born, he would get deathly sick from just a common cold. They said he had Bronchial Malesia and a very mild case of cystic Fibrosis (which to this day I am still not convinced he had) that they said he would outgrow.

He almost died more times than I could ever count; but I am certain he has a very strong reason for being here!

Honestly, every time we would have the priest come and read him his "Last rites" ... like magic the kid would get better and gain his health again!

The very last time he ever got sick it was like something out of a story book.

Most wouldn't believe it who weren't there... but I was there that day!

Due to his levels of illness, he had been transferred to a bigger hospital. He needed to be intubated and the hospital we were originally at couldn't do the level of care that it was taking just to keep him alive.

After he was transferred, I called his Father (who I had been split up from for several years already) and told him he had better hurry up if he wanted to see his son one last time.

I called "Father Mike" who was the new priest at the church I grew up in and I called my parents.

Although I had decided years ago to decline the Catholic religion; this priest was open minded and loved everyone no matter what.

He was the one who had baptized my sick infant son a couple of years prior in an emergency situation and then again in the church.

I had so much respect for this priest. More than I ever thought I would for any priest.

As I stood there beside the bed of my 5-year-old son; who was barely clinging to life; I deeply thought about the out of body experience I had on the day I gave birth to him.

I wondered if that was what it meant... that I would only get to have this child in my life for a little while... and then he would walk beside me as an angel?

I didn't know what to think... I was devasted.

My family arrived, and the priest walked in. Like many other times before, we all knew the drill... We would have no other choice than to say goodbye to this very sick little boy who would finally get the peace he deserved in Heaven.

Part of me felt relief for him, because he had been through so much in his short life! However, the mother in me wondered why I was cursed for having the family I always wanted... Because once again it would be ripped away.

The man I had been with for a couple of years at that point held me tightly as I fell into his arms.

We made a circle around the bed and we all held hands.

The nursing staff left the room to give us the respect of saying goodbye in private.

The priest began to pray with us as we all sobbed. He read my son his last rites and handed the little boy's soul over to Jesus to go to Heaven in peace!

I leaned over to hug my dying little boy... I felt his life force leaving his body and I knew that was it!

I whispered in his little ear "I have always loved you and always will. Fly high with the angels now baby. I will never let you go in my heart!"

Now, normally a mother would hit the floor out of absolute weakness in the knees after saying words like that to her 5-year-old son.

But it seemed as if as soon as I said that to him, something within his soul awoke. I can't explain in human terms what happened in the moments that followed. I just know what I felt.

If ever there were a true and real miracle that happened right in front of my own 2 eyes, this was it! If you were not there to witness it, you would probably not believe it; but several of us witnessed it.

Like a flash, the room seemed to get really bright and out of nowhere, my baby boy sat up in the bed... Looked around at all of us who were standing around him... And smiled.

"He's ok?" someone shouted.

"Did God hear our prayers? is he going to be ok?" someone else yelled out.

"Hit the nurse button! Call the Doctors, it's a miracle" … I heard a 3rd voice say.

I leaned in and hugged my fragile baby boy so hard. Still to this day I do not know what happened, but the best way I can explain it is to say that it was like his little being just decided to live.

As I held my precious bundle in my arms, he looked up at me and said, "Can I please watch Toy Story?"

It was a true miracle.

The doctors couldn't even explain it… neither could any of us who witnessed it!

All I can say is that within an hour of that happening, he was up and playing and left the hospital the next day!

He has never ever been sick since and it was like someone in the higher realms flipped a switch! Unexplainable and unbelievable to most!

That was the day that I truly began to believe in the power of the Holy Spirit and the true presence of God, the Universe, and the Divine.

There should have been no way that little boy should have been able to just sit up and over power death like that; but he did. I saw it happen and so did several others that day!

After that day I wondered in the back of my mind if my son was truly an angel walking around in Human's body.

The things he could do that no one else realized but me... The things he said only to me when he was a child that I never shared with anyone were all puzzle pieces that seemed to add up more and more.

One day, when he was 6, he told me that me and him and his sister were not from here! He told me that the 3 of us are not really Humans; but that we came from a place where everything is good and happy.

He told me "Me, my sister, and my mom... that's you... Came to Earth to help the people!"

I just thought it was a cute little imaginative statement at the time; but have since pondered many different meanings of it.

I asked him "Are we angels? From Heaven?"

To which he replied, "I think maybe... when we aren't Human, we have wings Momma... beautiful sparkly wings!"

I thought to myself what a wonderful mind this baby boy has! If only he knew how amazing I think he and his sister are!

When I think back to the days of my children being little; I am reminded how magical my offspring truly are!

My Daughter said some very profound things too when she was little!

One day when my beautiful daughter was 3, she told me all about the place that she came from. Where the streets are Gold and shiny".

I still to this day have never shared any of this with either of them as adults.

Neither of them knows the things I would see in visions or have been reminded of the conversations we had when they were little. I am not sure if they remember it, but when they read this book, I am sure it will spark something within their beings!

How can I be loved if I do not love myself? (Age 21-30)

24

CHAPTER

The Struggle was real

SINCE I KIND of got a bit ahead of myself in the last chapter, let me back up a bit so that you don't miss out on some of the most significant things that have been pieces of my spiritual puzzle.

So, by the age of 21, I was a mother of 2 very young babies. I had been working as a C.N.A for a couple of years and was in school to get my associates degree in Pharmacy.

Life was pretty good for a little bit and I stopped having too many "mystical" experiences for a couple of years (not sure why … it just was).

I knew that if I wanted to make a good name for myself that I must work hard and be the best mother I knew how to be. I knew that out of anything in the entire world, my children would always be the number one thing to me.

I never ever wanted my children to feel the way I felt as a child. I never ever wanted them to feel like they didn't have somewhere where they belonged.

I was determined to make sure my children had somewhere to be where they were loved and cherished.

I lived my life to make sure that I was their someone who would always fill them back up every time life had emptied their cups.

I was almost too obsessed at the time with being the perfect mother, the perfect wife, the perfect co-worker, the perfect person.

In my young adult life back then, I had already been through more than I had ever wanted my children to see.

I figured if I did a really good job with life that life would do a really good job of being good to me in return.

I dreamed of the day when I would feel like I belonged to a family; my own family.

I had that with my 2 children, but no one else.

Things with my son's Father started to become very hard and we really were not getting along very well for a very long time.

Since I had already been divorced once at such a young age from my daughter's father, I did not wat to be a failure again and I tried everything I could to make it work.

Unfortunately, his drinking became a very sore source of trouble between us.

We moved to another town to try and have a fresh start after he had put his hands on me and the police were called by the neighbors on night.

We both were very hopeful that if we moved for a fresh start, then maybe we could get along better. Both of us young and naive to the fact that if you don't get along in one home, chances are that moving to a new one will not improve things!

In spite of our young minded thinking that we could sweep things under the rug, things continued to get worse.

I came home one night after being at Volley Ball league and he was very drunk and angry.

He had written me a letter, telling me that he would change, he would stop drinking, and that we would be together forever.

I knew when I got home that night that something bad was about to happen; I felt it coming…I could just sense it.

I told him that I would like him to sleep on the couch and we would talk in the morning when he had sobered up.

I locked myself in the bedroom and laid my head down to get some rest. I knew my two young babes were sound asleep and I was angry with him that he was so drunk while taking care of my kids.

I did not want my kids to grow up in alcoholism like I did. I did not want my kids to live a life of chaos and darkness like I did.

I went to bed feeling extremely enraged that life had once again brought alcohol in as a poison in my close love relationships!

As I lay there thinking deeply about which was worse ... this or being a single mother?

He woke up and started banging on the bedroom door.

"Let me in!" he screamed.

"Stop!" I said ... "please just stop and go to bed! We will talk in the morning!"

"You are my wife and I have every right to sleep next to you. Let me in!" he yelled.

At that point I knew either way it wasn't going to be a good situation.

"The kids are sleeping ... Stop!" I yelled back

The next thing I knew, he stuck a knife through the bedroom door and broke the lock ;And let himself in.

He held me down in the bed with the knife to my throat. He told me if I didn't want to be with him, then I would be dead.

I played along with his game as I knew in that circumstance, it would be better than having a knife to my throat.

I did not want the kids waking up. I did not want my kids to know or sense or feel anything going on.

I told him I was sorry and that he was right, so he would stop. I just wanted him to stop. I just wanted it all to stop.

The next day I went to work and told a friend about what happened the night before. She said "You know you need to get a restraining order right?"

I didn't know what to do. I wanted out but was tired of failing at everything in life by that point!

For the safety of my children, I went on my lunch break and got a restraining order and had him met with the police when he came home from work that afternoon.

They assisted him to get some of his belongings and leave the premises.

That was a very hard day and although I knew life would be challenging and I knew I would have to find a second job to take care of everything on my own. Somehow, I felt it was better than ever subjecting my children to that ever again.

I cannot deny though, that deep down inside, I once again felt like a hue failure in the "Family" department.

I just was not meant to have a loving family, I guess.

People all around me were judging me for being a single mother of 2 kids and although I knew they were judging me; I also knew they had no clue what the truth was and all I cared about was making sure my kids were ok.

Deep inside I felt strongly like I didn't deserve true love; or to be loved by others.

I had yet to feel truly loved and cherished as I felt about my kids.

Shortly after that, I graduated from Pharmacy School and worked really hard to be a good and loving mommy and provider.

I started going out on weekends with my friends a lot for the first time since I had my daughter.

Yes, I had gone out, but this was starting to be every weekend.

Any chance I got, I started to leave my kids with my parents on weekends so I could just go do my own thing.

I didn't have any love for myself anymore. I secretly wanted to die. There were times when I thought maybe everyone would be better off if I just disappeared.

In fact, I truly didn't respect myself at all.

No matter what I had ever tried to do, it always went wrong.

No matter how good I tried to be, bad things just kept happening.

I couldn't see the blessing in anything anymore. I couldn't feel my angels around me. I hadn't seen my "Friends" in such a long time, I figured they must have given up on me too!

25
CHAPTER

Bleeding Love

I SPENT A god majority of my time deep thinking during the days and nights that followed my 2nd divorce.

I tried my very best to pick up the shattered pieces of my soul and try to make sense of everything that had been my life so far.

I dreamed about a day when I would find true love. I hadn't completely given up; and besides, it was not that big of a deal to be by myself with my children.

Although I was going out with friends every weekend, during the weekdays, I was devoted to my 2 beautiful children who I just adored.

At least, I had their love and they thought I hung the moon. I was over joyed just being in their presence.

I got myself to the point where I truly started to believe in love again and I wanted to give it one last chance.

It was almost like I could sense that a new man was about to enter my life. Just like the many times before when I just seemed to know these things without knowing how I knew; this was no exception!

One weekend a couple months later, I went out with friends and met the man that would forever change me.

When we met, he showed me love like I had never ever experienced. He brought me into his family, which was a very loving and united family unit.

I was loved, respected, cherished.

My children were too.

I was so thankful. I finally found my family I had been looking for!

The next 5 years would end up being some of the best years of my life.

Everything was more than perfect! The perfect husband who loved me and my children. They called him "Daddy".

The perfect job at the. Hospital making medicines for people.

The perfect "Family" life at home and who could ask for more!

I finally did it! I finally found it! It finally happened!

I fit in! I was a part of something, and it felt fantastic!

I started going to church every Sunday at a Methodist church down the street and I fit in there too!

I started seeing angels again when I went to church. I suddenly started having dreams of that baby boy angel again.

Then when I was just in the midst of the perfect life; I got pregnant!

I was so excited! This time would be different! This time with a man who I was married to!

This time I was older and had a great job, a beautiful house, and what I thought at the time was everything!

The kids were excited! My husband and I were absolutely ecstatic!

It was the 4th of July and we headed down to my husband's parent's house to join in on the festivities of the Parade and BBQ we did with them every year for the fourth!

When I got in the car that morning, I couldn't explain it, but I felt like something was wrong. I couldn't quite place it, and I sure didn't want to interrupt the high energy of the day for everyone, so I ignored all of the signs I was seeing that told me to slow down.

We got to the parade and we stood on the side of the road, excited for the kids to catch candy!

It was an extremely hot July day in Wisconsin. Although everything within me was telling me that I should take shelter in the shade and grab a glass of ice water.

Instead, I rushed around trying to help everyone get ready for the big parade! The kids were so excited, I did not have it in me to let them down.

How could I, they were my everything and this parade meant everything to all of us!

I assisted my little boy as he finished decorating and preparing his bike for the parade. Then I continued to help my baby girl put the perfect finishing touches on her little pink bike that she would ride in the parade too.

When the bikes were just right for riding, my husband kissed me goodbye and then took the 2 children to where the parade would start.

I watched as the three of them walked and rode away; anticipating how excited they would be when they saw Momma on the sidewalk waving as they rode by.

My children had given me strict instructions on how I should collect candy for them, since they were riding in the parade and wouldn't be there to fill their bags up.

I grabbed their candy bags and started walking towards the area where I knew all of the mothers would be meeting up to watch the parade.

As I walked, I started to feel very sick; dizzy, weak, and just off.

Although I had no idea what was going on, I still continued to ignore the warnings that were telling me to sit down!

I was tough, this was probably just pregnancy in the heat. I had been here before, so I decided to get myself a big drink of water and relax for a bit.

When I approached my then Mother in Law, she was staring at me with the strangest face I have ever seen her make.

"What's wrong?" I asked her?

She grabbed the empty chair next to her and in a Motherly voice said "Sit! You look exhausted and my unborn grandchild needs you to take a break. It's hot!"

I smiled and graciously accepted the chair; sat down for a minute and had a nice cold drink of water.

Within a few minutes, the parade was headed our way and I could see my beautiful babies off in the distance headed my way.

I stood up to get a much closer view of them; and of course, to catch some candy for them for later as promised.

As I stood up, I felt faint again; but continued to try and ignore it. I was tough, I just needed to get through this parade and then I could relax.

I walked towards the street and bent over, scooped up a fairly large pile of candy laying in the street that the children around me missed.

Suddenly, I felt something running down my leg.

I ran to find a bathroom and couldn't believe my eyes. I thought to myself. "Blood? Oh No, God Please No!"

I could not deny that had blood running down my leg. It wasn't a whole lot, but none the less it was there.

I cleaned up and then hurried back so I didn't miss my kids riding by.

When I got back to the parade, I didn't say a word to anyone as I sure didn't want to ruin the fun everyone was having.

The last thing I wanted to do was to scare people if this was just from the heat.

I mean, I knew from my own experience being pregnant and from the many other friends of mine who have had babies; that sporadic vaginal bleeding happens when women are pregnant all the time.

I watched my children as they rode by on their bicycles; waving and shouting "Mommy!".

I smiled and waved back; blowing them kisses and telling them what a wonderful job they were doing.

"This must be something that dreams are made of", I thought to myself as I watched my loving and supportive husband follow very close behind my two precious babies.

As I saw how much he seemed to love them and how filled with joy they were to be riding in the parade; I felt so much gratitude. I felt like I was in the best dream of my life in that moment.

The moments of pure bliss that I felt just then filled me up with so much love.

The parade ended shortly after that and we headed back to my in-law's house to make food.

I went to the bathroom and I could no longer deny the fact that I was profusely bleeding everywhere.

I called out for my husband to come in the bathroom.

"I am bleeding" I told him.

"How bad is it? Are you ok?" he asked

"It's pretty bad. I have been trying to ignore it, but it's not going away?" I explained

"We better go to the hospital huh?" he asked.

"yeah I guess", I said as I could feel my spirit sinking. I just knew what was happening. I could feel it.

On the way to the hospital, I saw that little baby angel again. I hadn't seen him in a very long time, but he was there again.

When we got to the Emergency room, we were taken immediately back to a private room.

The Emergency room doctor followed us in to the room and wasted no time giving me a thorough gynecological exam.

As I lay there on my back, I watched every move he had. I could see out of the corner of my eye, all of the blood that was all over the table, his gloves and tools, and myself.

I saw the look on his face when he was finished and pulled his gloves off.

Somehow, I already knew what he was going to say; but somewhere in my being I hoped that I was wrong.

He looked me straight in the eye, and said "I am so sorry, but you are having a miscarriage!"

I desperately said "Are you sure? Can we stop it?"

I watched him take a deep breath and compassionately say "Unfortunately, it's too late. I am so sorry!"

At that point I was so tired of everything good in my life turning into something awful and I was just tired of everything!

I had no words. I had no explanation for the way I felt.

Why does this always happen to me? I wondered.

Just when things go very right, why do they have to begin to go very wrong?

None of it made any sense in the moments, days, and even weeks that followed the miscarriage.

The 2-hour drive home from my in-law's house the next day was in silence.

Neither of us knew what to say to each other.

Our marriage was never the same after that day.

Although, I still cannot explain it, I could just feel it; the magic was lost.

I am not sure what it was about a miscarriage that takes the power of love away; but it happened.

After the tragic loss of our unborn child, the love between us was just gone!

26
CHAPTER

The Sinking Ship

THE DAYS, WEEKS, and months following the miscarriage would prove to me once again that at that point in my life; no matter how good of a person I was, I could not control fate.

About 2 weeks after I lost my unborn baby, they found a tumor the size of a grapefruit on my left ovary and I ended up having emergency surgery.

The Cancer was back, and it was not holding back this time. It was not only on my cervix, but it had reached my ovaries and my Uterus as well.

I was once again losing everything, it seemed.

Even though I had found the perfect life, the darkness once again began to find the perfect time to take away my light. Again!

After surgery, I lost my left ovary, but they said they got any and all cancer cells and I once again gained a clean bill of health ...

They told me that I would not be able to carry another child to term though.

I could feel my ship sinking the day I was told I would lose my "womanhood" against my will.

After I healed from surgery, my husband told me one day that he wasn't sure if he could deal with me not being able to have any more kids.

Those words radiated throughout my whole being as I sat there feeling like I must be the biggest failure that the Universe had ever seen.

I was always able to have children; this had never been a problem in the past, obviously.

So why? Why now? Why when I had the perfect marriage, the perfect family, the perfect life would that be taken from me?

I must have done way too much wrong in my life and I just knew I must be serving a higher sentence.

I could feel darkness radiating all throughout and around my soul.

I was so hurt by my husband's words that, that I think looking back now, I put an immediate wall up between him and I.

Everything in my life felt like it had become out of control once again. Through no fault of my own, I had been stripped of the one thing that makes a woman magical; having children.

I started to give up on life. I mean seriously, who has that many ups and downs?

By this time in my life, I should be further along in success. I must truly just be worthless. I sure felt like it.

I began going out with friends again and I didn't care at all. I was tired of caring. I had enough of being throat punched by life.

I started blowing off work to sleep in when the nights got too long.

I stopped coming home at night when I did go out. Many mornings would find myself waking up in every home but my own.

By the time my husband had realized how badly he hurt me with his words and apologized; it was too late. I had already moved away from him. I had already disconnected from him.

I felt deep inside that I would be holding him back if I kept him locked up in the clutches of my sinking ship.

I mean, I had been a basket case my entire life.

I was not even wanted by my own parents, so how did I think such a wonderful man would want to be with me when I can't even give him the one thing, he wanted most in the world; a child!

I felt like I didn't deserve him. He was the best thing that had ever happened to me and my children; but yet, I just knew I had to let him go!

He deserved to be with a real woman who could carry his children.

I told him all of that and he tried to talk me down from the ledge; but the feeling in my soul was so strong!

Who was I to make him stay with me and rob him of the experience of having a child of his own?

I knew that he loved my 2 children like they were his own, without a shadow of a doubt.

But I felt so deeply like I had to let him go ... for his own good. I knew he would not ever understand that, and I couldn't make him understand.

I knew that I had no choice ... I started staying away longer and longer from home.

I started sleeping in the living room, I started the process of letting him go.

I knew somewhere in my being that I had to hurt him to make him go away; because he was the one person in the world that loved me without conditions.

It was so hard to do, and I loved this man more than life itself; but I did not want to be selfish and take his opportunity to have his own child away from him.

Long story short, he ended up meeting a girl, falling in love, and having 2 beautiful children of his own.

So, I was so happy years later that I followed the strong calling to let him go; even though I loved him like I had never loved another.

Even though, for the first time in my life, I was complete … I was happy. I was loved … I had a "Family".

I prayed that I would someday be rewarded for the selfless act. Although it did not appear selfless to those around me who only saw me pushing him away.

I truly did it for his own good. Or what I thought was at the time.

27

CHAPTER

Dancing with the Devil

AS I STILL believe today, back then I was following my intuition very strongly. I followed the strong callings and feelings that I felt deep inside, no matter who didn't understand.

I am sure I must have looked really awful to those that were not walking in my shoes during those days; but I sincerely know that the man who loved me without condition was not meant to walk beside me forever.

He was only there for a season and I will be forever grateful for that beautiful life me and the kids lived with him.

I was very sick for a long time after we split up and I moved out.

In the next several years, I would end up being diagnosed with female cancer yet again (to the point where I ended up with a full hysterectomy at 28), thyroid problems, Fibromyalgia, Degenerative Disc Disease and MS.

I figured that must have been meant to be, since I had been through so much in my young life already. I must have been meant to be sick.

I was glad that I didn't put that good man through all of the nonsense of dealing with me and my health problems!

He deserved better than being with me. What did I have to offer, but a sick wife!

In the year after our divorce, I started dating a man that I thought would be my saving grace from everything.

But in all reality, he ended up being a huge fall from grace!

Throughout the years, I had been on again/off again with my parents and siblings.

Depending on which guy I was dating, would depend on which family members would accept me or not.

Well, while I dated this guy; we will call him Satin for the sake of this book … because I truly thought I was dancing with the Devil himself at times.

This guy, Satin … Was one of the most manipulative people I have ever met in the entire world.

He was so good at his game that by the time I realized he had me in his spider web, everyone around me had already ran away.

But when you are with a true manipulator, you are the last one to see it.

I went from having the best years of my life to having the worst year of my life that I had up to that point.

As I always had, I finally pulled myself back into my own light after all of the trauma I went through with losing my paradise.

I was 3 months away from being 30 years old. My kids were doing great; My career was amazing.

Life was great. I had pulled through and overcame obstacles, once again that most people can't even begin to understand.

Except for the things going on all around me that I was too blind to see.

"Satin" talked me into putting a drywall company in my name for him, because according to him and his sob story; the mother of his children destroyed his credit and he couldn't have it in his name as she would take it away from him in child support.

I didn't just stop there though. Oh no, not me! I went ahead and put everything in my name for this guy.

I think that I was still in the energy of that unconditional love I felt from my last relationship and without knowing I was doing it, I think because I had been treated with so much love in my last relationship, I somehow felt it was my duty to turn around and bless someone else's path this time.

From homes to credit cards to bank accounts ... to utility bills; you name it and it was in my name to make things a little easier for this man!

Even though, the heart of me wanted to help this man, as I felt so sorry for him and all that he had been put through by others; The human part of me never felt completely comfortable about putting my good name in jeopardy of losing my reputation.

Although I wrestled with the angels on my left and the devil on my right shoulder; the lost and broken and abandoned inner child within me figured it was the best that I deserved, and I should just be thankful that someone wanted to be with me.

Shortly after I started dating Satin ... I started having mystical experiences again. I assumed it was because I had been so sick and maybe I was going to die soon (at that point I truly thought I deserved to ... I was never truly wanted by anyone except my kids and my husband that I had just let go a few short years before).

I started to see my "friends" around my bed side at night again and I started to see spirits everywhere I went.

I could see them walking around. in and out and through buildings and people.

I continued still at that point to keep it to myself. I must have really been mentally messed up from all the traumas in my life.

I really believed at that time that it must have been my imagination getting the best of me again!

At least that is what I had always been told; so, I believed it!

I mean, "Satin" told me all the time how awful I was and that I would never deserve anything of substance in my life …

I was emotionally beat down to the point where I couldn't even see my own spirit anymore. I had no self-worth at all, and I could never imagine getting it back at that point.

In fact, Just like when I was with my Son's Father, I started to see dark spirits and shadows around this guy at night when we slept.

But at that time, I didn't question it. I assumed I must be the problem, I seemed to have such bad luck that maybe I was the problem all along.

I truly believed I was the bad spirit!

I had left the bad relationship with him after he gave me 2 black eyes one night for no reason at all, other than he was mad at someone else.

I got out, and went to stay with my Sister Tammy. For the 2nd time in my life, she was my saving Grace!

When I went to stay with her, she sat me down and told me that everyone knew I was being abused.

She explained to me that all the signs had been there for a very long time and no one knew what to do.

She was an AODA councilor for a living and worked with battered and abused women and Men.

She pulled out a "Cycle of Abuse" picture and told me I was being very badly manipulated.

But I told her she was exaggerating. I told her time and time again "You don't know him like I do!"

After all of her failed attempts to help me see how beautiful and deserving I was, I just couldn't see any other man wanting a washed up and sick girl like me.

I was mentally spent, I was physically ill and could hardly walk most day.

Who would want to be with someone like that? What man would ever want me?

I figured I should just be thankful that I had someone who wanted to share space with me. I mean, he says he loves me; shouldn't that be good enough for me?

What is wrong with me, I wondered. How could I be so ungrateful?

My family would never understand where I was coming from as they all had their own burdens, they were filled full of.

Once I realized it was probably my best option, I went back to him.

Not only because it was all I felt I deserved, but also because at the time it seemed easier then explaining myself to my family.

He had me so mind bent into believing that everyone around me was against me and he was the only one who truly cared about me.

I think because of everything I had been through with my parents through the years, it made it easy for me to believe him when he told me that my mother didn't even love me.

28

CHAPTER

My deadly mistake

ONE DAY, AFTER I took him back, my mom came over to our apartment, where Satin and her got into an absolutely awful altercation.

I was shunned from the family completely after that day, because I didn't stand up for my Mom enough.

However, I was not given the chance to explain myself either. I was just banished from existence in all of their worlds.

I shouldn't have let it bother me, because I already felt very unloved by all of them anyway. But it crushed me into even more pieces than I was already shredded into throughout the years.

If someone would have taken the time to hear me, I would have explained that personally, I didn't stand up for either of them.

I felt whole heartedly that they were both out of line and I tried to tell her that, but by the time she got home and told the story to my dad; I was hated within 15 minutes.

Once again, my family turned their backs on me even though I personally was not the one who did the damage.

I couldn't see the chips falling all around me though. He had everything just the way he liked it.

I had only him. He had me curled up in fetal position in the corner with no support from anyone else.

Little did I know at the time that Valentine's day in 2005 would end up taking me to the next level of Hell in my miserable existence!

I would go to places that I never thought were true in real life. If I thought I was in hell realms before; I had no idea what Hell truly was up until that point.

"Satin" had been acting increasingly angry for several weeks before that and I felt so strongly within my being that I was in danger.

But of course, those days I wasn't too keen on following my angels or my intuition since in my mind back then they had been failing me for far too long. I wasn't even paying attention anymore!

Looking back at it now, if I would have just known that my angels were trying to save my life, I am certain things may have played out a whole lot better.

I mean, I had a dream a few nights before that of a car crashing into a brick wall.

I saw signs all around me that told me to get away from him (but I didn't see it until it was too late).

So that night, we had plans to go out to eat and have a few drinks with friends.

He wanted me to stay at a hotel with him, but I couldn't because my 10-year-old son was home that night.

He was mad because I wasn't willing to leave my baby home alone all night.

I didn't even feel comfortable leaving him home alone for the few hours that we were going to go out.

But Satin insisted that we must to go out that night.

I felt like the worst Mother on the planet; as my child begged me … "Please momma, please don't go!"

I reassured him "We won't be one long, I promise. I will be home before you know it!!"

My son cried and begged one more time.

"I just don't feel safe here alone. Will you please stay home momma?"

Before I could even get a word out, Satin Yelled "He's a tit baby Momma's boy. He needs to grow up!"

I felt so torn. I didn't want to leave my son; I knew it wasn't a good idea!

But Satin was relentless and wasn't going to let this go!

I put a special movie on for him and gave him some snacks and then against everything I felt deep inside, I walked out that door.

We went to the bar where we would frequently hang out with friends and never went to dinner.

When we pulled up, I said "Aren't we going out for dinner?"

He gave me the evil eye and screamed at me "Don't question me!"

I watched as he became increasingly angry as the minutes passed.

After about an hour of him going in and out of the bar with some friends and ignoring me,

He walked up to me sitting at the bar by myself and whispered in my ear "You will be lucky if I don't kill you tonight!"

"What?" I said.

He laughed a very creepy laugh and walked away from me.

A few minutes later, he walked back up and said "I was just kidding, chill out!"

The next half hour he whispered "Die Bitch" in my ear several times.

After about 4 times of hearing such words, I leaned into the bartender and said "I am scared of him. He is saying some insane things to me that he has never said before!"

The bartender who was our friend, who I thought was an honest person told me,
"Oh he is just drunk, you are fine!"
I said, "You didn't hear what he said though! He told me he is going to kill me!"
He shook his head and walked away from me.
I grabbed my cell phone to call a cab to take me home, because I felt so strongly like something was very wrong.
Satin walked up to me at that moment and said "You Bitch! why are you telling lies about me to the bartender?"
I replied "They are not lies. You are truly scaring me! I want to go home"

He said "Let's go! NOW!"
Then he walked out the door, started my van up and drove up to the door of the bar.
One more time, I reached out to those around me and said "Please, someone help me. I don't feel safe leaving with him!"

The bartender sternly said, "just get in the van and go home with him, knock off the drama!"
I was so scared, like I had never been scared before. This was a whole new level of terror that I had never felt the energy of until those moments leading up to the drive home.

There is a whole lot that my brain had blocked out about what happened next; but I do remember getting into the van and him peeling out of the parking lot.

I know we pulled into a corn field and driving through the corn while he explained in detail how he was going to murder me and chop my body into pieces.

I am not certain what all happened after that, but the next thing I knew I woke up and saw that I was in my van and it was parked in front of the garage at our home.

I was in the passenger seat leaned up against the window.

Once I realized that I had been passed out, I sat up and immediately, saw blood dripping from the side of my head.

When I sat all the way up, I realized there was a huge blood stain on the window.

I leaned down and saw my cell phone laying on the floor by my feet and grabbed it.

My heart was racing and as I hurried to dial 911.

In what seemed like approximately 6 seconds, I felt the van door swing open.

He grabbed the phone and threw it on the ground outside and smashed it into thousands of pieces.

Next, he Grabbed me by my hair and threw me to the ground along with the smashed-up cell phone.

As soon as I realized we were home, I knew I had once choice and it was to fight for my life!

The thoughts came rushing to my mind that my child was in the house and it was like every single ounce of adrenaline in my frail body kicked into over-drive.

In the moments to follow, I found myself fighting back with all of my might to get away so I could get in the house and make sure my son was ok.

I ended up getting loose from his grip on me and ran to the house.

Just as I got up on the porch, he grabbed my head and smashed the back of it into the bricks on the front of the house.

I felt woozy and I thought I was going to fade out; but as soon as I thought about my son, it was like a momma bear type of thing and I would temporarily gain strength again.

I got away and with the rest of the strength I had left, I pushed my way into the house and called out for my child!

He came running into the kitchen where I stood and Just when I was about to say "Call 911";

Satin ran in the house and threw me to the floor once again.

He aggressively got on top of me and started just beating on me. I just kept feeling hit fist hitting my face over and over.

I could hear my child in the background screaming "Satin. No! Leave my Mom ALONE!"

My son somehow got a "911" call in before the home phone was ripped out of the wall too.

There had to have been some sort of Divine Intervention, because the next thing I knew, the house was surrounded in police cars!

Officers busted into the house, with guns drawn; just like you see on TV.

I laid there, feeling my life force leaving me. I went out of my body again.

I saw myself leave my body. I watched myself floating over top of my body this time.

As I floated up, I saw blood surrounding my whole body. it looked like a scene from a Hollywood movie.

I saw 2 flashes of light and then I saw the Yellow brick road again.

I stood there, looking around and this time I saw birds flying around everywhere.

I looked everywhere for someone. I mean I would have been happy to see anyone.

"Jesus? Are you here?" I called out.

But no one was there ...

I heard a voice calling out to me ...

"Maam?. ... Maaam?"

"What's her name?" I heard.
Then I heard "Yes, she belongs to me, she is my Momma!"

I opened my eyes and I saw my son sitting on the lap of a police officer who was doing his very best to calm the poor child.

I tried to sit up and another officer said, "Please, Maam, stay there, you are hurt very badly.
We aren't sure, but we think your neck is broken."
I just broke down and began to cry. I cried so hard. What had just happened? I lost it!
This was a new level of horrible.

What happened?

All I could think in that moment was "Lord, please, tell me my child was not touched!"

Even laying there on the floor, I could see my baby shaking so hard that he couldn't breathe very well.

We both ended up in an ambulance and headed to the hospital.

My child was not hurt physically, thankfully.

But he was traumatized to the point that he would never be the same again.

As if it wasn't bad enough that I had just been through something that was like the worst horror movie you could ever imagine.

And not to mention the fact that my child was put through way too much.

The icing on the cake was the fact that I had nobody to turn to … No one!

Once again, life had showed me how much I deserved (or so I thought at the time).

I could not even fathom what I could have possibly done to deserve this though.

I just couldn't understand it, not any of it!

I had been good to "Satin". I put myself all the way out there for him and I had his back when everyone else seemed to have turned on him

I was the one person, who he should be appreciative of; not angry with!

Why? …

Why did he act that like?

Why did he do this?

What did I do?

And the more I questioned it in my mind, the more I realized I had no idea truly what the deal was.

Since I had no one left in my life, my son had to hang out in the hospital with me until I was released the next day.

Thank goodness, my neck was not broken, but my heart and spirit sure were!

I had lots of bumps, bruises, scrapes, and some very nasty cuts on my head from glass and bricks; but in the bigger picture, I was going to be alright!

I had permanent scars on my heart that would not fade anytime soon; but I was used to that and I knew I would eventually recover.

When I was released from the hospital, they told me he was caught and put in jail and that the police had put a temporary restraining order on him.

So even if he was released from Jail, he was to have no contact with me until he went to court.

I took a taxi cab back home. It was just me and my baby. I just kept thinking about how thankful I was that we had both survived this.

I also kept feeling so grateful that my daughter was not home that weekend!

We pulled in the driveway and I looked over and saw my van had every single window smashed out of it.

There was glass everywhere! it was an awful scene!

After looking a little closer, I saw blood everywhere! My own blood, just everywhere!

We went inside the house, and at the kitchen table sat the bartender from that night and 2 other buddies of Satin's.

They had guns in their hands and said, "Grab a few belongings that you need for now and leave!"

I said, "This is my house and my stuff, I am not leaving!"

He held the gun up to my face and said, "I say you will be leaving, right now!"

I grabbed my child and we left with nothing!

Walked out the door, got into my van with the windows smashed out, In the middle of winter and drove out of the driveway!

Leaving behind everything I had worked hard for, for the last 13 Years.

Leaving behind every single baby picture I ever had of my children!

Leaving behind every single toy my children loved; their favorite blankies, their games!

Leaving everything behind except the shirts on our backs and a busted-up minivan.

I left with the bloody shirt I was wearing.

I had nowhere to go … No-one to turn to … nothing!

I was absolutely devastated!

I drove to my son's friend's house and asked his Mom if we could stay there for a few days until I got it all figured out!

Even though I didn't know her, and she didn't know me … I had to!

She was very compassionate of our situation and said too had been there before. We stayed there for a few nights until I got plans into place for safety for me and the kids.

It didn't take long, until the whole town was talking about what had happened.

I found out that the man I had been living with had gotten involved with a local drug selling gang behind my back.

They were into Meth very badly; and he was not only selling it but was using it.

It began to make sense finally; I figured that was why he acted to erratically!

And that's why the bartender turned his back on me like that; He was in it too!

I had hit a new low …
How could I not see all of this going on around me …
No wonder everyone else left me!
I had enough of having enough of everything!

29
CHAPTER

Playing with Fire

AS I BEGAN the gather the broken and shattered pieces of my life and my dreams once again, I ended up staying with friends here and there for short amounts of time.

However, as soon as I felt comfortable enough to open up about the truth of my situation, it wouldn't be very long before there would be an excuse made why the kids and I couldn't stay anymore.

I sure couldn't blame any of them, though. I am certain they weren't trying to ruin their lives, as I had with my bad choices.

I mean, no one wanted to deal with a Mom and 2 kids who were in hiding from a local gang and a man who was truly trying to kill her.

It was a very dangerous situation that I couldn't believe myself was even happening.

During my short stay at my friend Margaret's home; the kids and I shared a bedroom and shared everything.
As long as I had them and they had me, all would be well.
Or so I thought!

One weekend, my kids were gone, and I got invited to go on a motorcycle ride with a guy I had met in the bar the night before.

During those days when I didn't have my children with me, I would spend my time in the bar!

It kept my mind from real life, and it kept me socializing, because I didn't know how to process the raw emotions I was stuffing down with the alcohol.

I had never been a big drinker, but at this point, I felt like there was truly no point in spending my time being good anymore ... for what?

All these years spent trying to be such a good person and no matter what I did, bad things, people, and situations... pure darkness would always find me and ruin everything for me anyway!

So, what was the harm in going on a Motorcycle ride with a guy I barely knew?

Right?

The funny thing is that morning, I had a strong and strange feeling that I was going to regret my choice (as I typically did in those days it seemed); but I certainly wasn't going to listen to my intuition any more ... period!

It had never led me to the right place and time.

Besides, all it ever did was led me to embarrassment, and being rejected! So, I had decided that I was on a mission to do whatever my ego and anger said would be instant gratification for me.

So, I saddled up on the back of a Harley Davidson with a guy who thought I was amazing!

As the day went on and we met up with others, I noticed that there were people I grew up with in the group of riders!

Even more reason that I should be here today, I thought ... speaking of signs!

This must have been meant to be! Oh, what fun we would have!

We drove around stopping at bar after bar and drinking more and more throughout the day.

In the afternoon, we headed out toward Spring Green, WI; where the roads were curvy, and the scenery was spectacular!

We were on a big curve to the left and I will never forget the moment when the bike next to us rushed to the inside of us in the midst of the curve.

I felt the handlebar of that bike hit our gas tank ... Dead center!

In what felt like a slow motion of very few moments in time.

I watched as I flew up and over the top of the bike, which was going 55MPH at that moment in time!

I saw myself flying through the air! I felt the wind beneath me, and then like a flash, I saw something out of the corner of my eye.

"Here I go again ..." I thought to myself in that moment.

I saw what appeared to be lights flashing all around me and I hit the ground hard!

I instantly began rolling uncontrollably from the force that I was thrown with.

Suddenly, I noticed that the flashes of light were in fact a controlled burn going on in the ditch.

As soon as I realized what was going on, it hit me that I was headed straight for that fire; full force!

With all of the might I could muster up in a few seconds of time, I did everything I could to stop myself from heading into that fire!

My life flashed before my eyes and I just knew I was going to die! From what my eyes were seeing, there was no way possible for me to get out of this one, this time!

I began to feel the heat of the fire all around me. I felt the energy of the raging fire I was about to be burned alive in.

In that moment, the memories of the flames from the fire that had almost taken my life at 3 years old rushed back to my mind for a second or two.

What was the significance of this? There has to be meaning. This is not typical in everyone's lives.

Not everyone has these extreme circumstances. I am not sure why I am constantly chosen to go through this. Why me?

Those were the questions that were running through my mind as I felt the heat getting closer and closer to my body.

Just as I was beginning to land in the fire, because I lost control and strength enough to stop myself anymore.

Just as I braced myself for death and had accepted my fate; in the very next moment, something happened that I will never forget.

As if the hand of God picked me up from the fire of hell and placed me where I belonged; I felt an unknown force that I still to this day cannot explain … pick me up and carry me backwards!

As I felt my whole Human body cradled and carried to safety, I then felt the force drop me on the ground again!

Just as I felt the force of my body hitting the ground for a second time, I saw myself leave my body.

I once again floated high above my physical existence.

I watched as people were running over and gathered around my lifeless body.

I heard a very loud voice say to me …
"Are you done feeding external fires?"

In that moment, I opened my eyes and looked up at the crowd gathered around me, and I heard someone say, "She's awake ... Are you ok?"

I laid there and felt excruciating pain in my entire body. I knew this time I was hurt badly again.

There should have been no way that I should have been able to sit up, stand up, and walk away from that accident.

I knew many who had perished in motorcycle accidents going much slower.

As I got up, I was told that I couldn't go to the hospital, because the guy I was riding with didn't have a driver's license.

"Please just keep this to yourself!" he begged of me!

At that point, I was so happy to be ok, That I let it go!

Although I would end up having to get medical attention and lie about what happened; I ended up having to pay my own medical bills as well.

It dawned on me about a week later that I was given signs that told me to steer clear of the situation, but I didn't listen to them.

Another incident that I could have prevented, if I had just trusted in my own gut feelings!

I began to wonder if that is what my lessons were in all of this nonsense that just wouldn't stop happening to me.

Why was I saved though? I had almost nothing left to offer the world anymore.

I figured it must be so that my children could have their mother, and I decided that I would start making better choices going forward.

30
CHAPTER

Desperado come
to your senses

I KNOW AFTER everything I had experienced in the first few generations of my life, I truly started to see that all of this heavenly guidance and assistance that I had received was not appreciated.

Not that I didn't appreciate it, but because in my Humanness, I truly didn't understand it. And to be very honest, I didn't really believe in it fully.

I still secretly wondered if it was my imagination. I still could hear everyone else's words radiating through my being, telling me that there was no such thing as Heaven and there was no such thing as angels.

I had been through hell in my life, more than anyone else I had even known.

So, was it because I wasn't listening to my higher calling? Was it because I was going against what my soul wanted me to accomplish in this life?

Was I missing the boat completely?

I wondered these things over and over and over.

I decided at that point that I needed to just take things one day at a time and see what else would be shown to me.

I did, however, promise myself that I would try harder to listen to what my gut feelings were telling me, even if I didn't believe in them.

But for a while, it just seemed like, no matter how hard I tried, it was like I just couldn't get anything right.

I ended up in the hospital with alcohol poisoning a few weeks later, when I decided it was a great idea to do 30 Yaeger bombs for my 30th birthday.

Eventually all of my friends around me decided that they had enough, and Margaret was raising little children and told me to get out after that!

I ended up homeless once again, but this time, I lost everything I had ever owned.

I was living in my busted-up van and because I loved my children more than life itself;

I ended up having to make a choice that I never ever wanted to make.

I had to do what was best for my kids and let them go live with their dads.

There was no way on God's Green Earth that I was going to continue to let them be in harm's way living with me.

There was no way in hell I was going to let them live in my broken-down van with me either.

These 2 Angels were such precious gifts to the world, and I had ruined their lives for long enough.

I had to do what was right and help them to find stability once again, even if I couldn't find it for myself.

It was one of the worst days of my life.

I will never forget the screams that came from my children as I sat them down to explain to them that it would only be for a little while.

Just until Mom can find somewhere safe for us to live without danger.

When I drove away that night, I truthfully, more than any other time in my life, wanted to die!

I felt like I just couldn't keep going. I had ruined everything!

I had no one ... nothing ... not even my children; No reason for living anymore!!!

I leaned the seat back in my van that night ... and prayed ... cried ... And screamed;

"God ... Why are you doing this to me? What have I done to deserve this life I have lived ...? I have always tried to do my best ... but I can't catch a break!!!"

"GOD I AM SO MAD AT YOU!!!" I yelled so loudly1

I just couldn't comprehend how me of all people could lose my children ...

I mean, drug addicts lose their children ... and alcoholics lose their children ...

People who don't care about their babies ... lose them ...

I had worked so hard to stay away from drugs ... and I hardly ever drank Alcohol most of my life due to what I went through as a child!

And I cared selflessly about my babies ...

So why? Just Why?

For the next few weeks, I went to work every day, and no one there had any clue I was homeless.

I would shower at the truck stop and then go to work each day.

At work they would talk about what they were going to do afterwards and I would try to find something really busy to do to avoid the conversations.

I dreaded when it was over at 4pm; because, I knew it meant I would have 16 hours of sitting in my van.

I just couldn't take it anymore. Why did I always try to be such a good person? What was I trying to prove?

No matter what good I did in the world, I always kept ending up in circumstances beyond my control that would leave me scratching my head and wondering what happened!

The sting of all the years of hurt, rejection, anger, abandonment, and shame for what I had become really started to build up!

I started getting drunk every weekend, just to pass the time until I could get my children back.

I was drinking more than I had ever before.
I recognized it, but I just truly didn't care anymore!
I hoped that I would die from it.
I tried several times to die from it … I wanted to die!

For the first time in my life, I was doing any drug that was offered to me, along with alcohol, just to numb the pain!

I started hanging out with an old friend who lived close to where I was sleeping in my van.

It didn't take long for him to introduce me to Crack Cocaine; so, I started mixing that with alcohol too!

I never did it during the week when I went to work; but on weekends … It was no holds barred!

Every time I got intoxicated, I hoped I wouldn't wake up!

I mean, my own family didn't want me, so what was the point? My kids were barely around me either.

I was not a good person anymore ... I lost my spark ... I couldn't find my "Friends" and I stopped feeling any sort of connection to God!

I was so lost and honestly, I think the shadow side of me began to embrace the darkness of being and feeling lost.

I was so angry. Anger just seethed through my internal being. I felt as though I was a huge wood tick, just ripe for popping.

Or as some people like to say, I felt like a busted can of biscuits. I felt like one little poke was going to cause the ultimate explosion.

I did worry about what would happen if I did end up exploding. I knew what I was capable of, from my earlier days of being a "bad girl" and fighting until the other person called uncle.

I did so much deep thinking all of those hours I spent in my van. I wondered if I was being punished for the days of beating other girls up as a teenager.

It was quite confusing though, because when I thought about being punished for my actions; my thoughts would immediately take me back to the woods at the farm when I was a little girl and I was bight and sparkly and shiny and happy!

I was innocent and couldn't have possibly caused those bad things to happen to me that created my original anger, could I?

When I tried to make it make sense, it would spin in another direction. I would go from victim, to aggressor, to angel and then back to Devil.

It seemed to me that no matter what, I was in such a strong spider web of thoughts and emotions that I would get extremely overwhelmed and then I would drink to numb it all up.

I would spend time walking the beaches in Madison, for hours, because somehow, I could feel that the water was healing for my mind.

Life had made me hard at that point and when I say hard, I mean stubborn and angry. I was at the point in my life where I had nothing left to lose.

I had lost everything and everyone that had ever mattered to me.

Just trying to make sense of it all would make me feel extreme overwhelm.

I wondered over and over; "Why am I here?"

I had begun to believe that life had been nothing but one fight after another for me. It seemed like even when I was following the light and connected with my soul, something or someone else would come along and screw up my progress; bump me off my path.

Even though there were times when I thought about leaving my van running with me in it or swimming out to the middle of Lake Mendota and just disappearing; I had even stronger thoughts that would take their place and tell me that I needed to keep going.

I would feel a strong pull to not give up.

I was having the same dream almost every night when I slept in my van.

I vividly dreamed about angels and Heaven. I would see visions of myself standing at a podium and speaking to a large crowd.

In the dream, the crowd was looking up to me and they all wanted me to help them feel better within their own lives.

They were looking to me to help them make sense of their own troubles.

Of course, the dream was very confusing to me, because I thought "how could people possibly look up to me? I cannot even look up to my own self right now!"

I could just feel that things were about to change in my life again, but I had no idea that I was about to hit "Rock Bottom".

31
CHAPTER

My Ultimate Rock Bottom

SPEAKING OF "ROCK bottom" I recall so clearly the morning that I hit rock bottom very well.

With all that I had been doing, I guess I had to figure there would be a rock bottom, right?

We always hear that someone hit rock bottom, and when it happened to me, I knew right away!

That morning, I woke up in the passenger seat of my broken-down van; in front of the house of the friend of mine who introduced me to crack cocaine.

I looked down and I had emptied both my bladder and bowels all over myself; and when I went to move, I noticed I have vomited everywhere too.

"What the heck happened?" I wondered to myself.

I just couldn't remember anything from the night before, but all I knew was a had a couple of beers and then things seemed to black out.

I knocked on the door of my friend's house and I asked him, "What is going on? Why am I in front of your house? Who drove me home?" amongst many other questions going through my mind.

He looked at me with disgust and said, "Well let's just say you are lucky you are not in jail right now. You went way too far last night and by the way, the police are looking for you!"

"Oh my God! … what?" I exclaimed.

"Yeah, we went to an after-bar party last night and there was a girl standing in the corner of the room when we walked in the door. For what seemed like no reason at all, you flew across the room and just attacked her! You threw her down to the ground and beat on her until she went unconscious!"

I was paralyzed for a moment, as I tried to figure out why I would do such a thing? It wasn't me, not my nature. Not usually!

All I could think was there had to be more to the story. I know myself. I may be angry and lost right now, but I cannot imagine that I would ever take my aggression out on an innocent person like that.

Had I lost my mind finally? What had I done? I know when I was younger and would get into physical fights with other girls, it was always when I was provoked; it was always because I was defending myself.

So, this was a new low for me and I felt it deeply inside.

"Oh my God… I have become a horrible person!" I thought to myself.

Just when I began to catch my breath, my friend looked me straight in the eye and said, "Oh and yeah, she is in the hospital as we speak. Between that and the police actively looking for you, I didn't bring you in the house last night. I left you out there so that if they came for you, it wouldn't affect me!"

"Are you serious?" I said.

"You didn't want me to affect you?" I asked.

"Well yeah, I have drugs silly. I wasn't going down because you are stupid drunk!" he replied.

"Do you know what hospital she is in? Do we know her name?" I asked.

"Yep, I have all the info here" … he said as he handed me a piece of paper.

"Remember, not my problem; Its yours!" he reminded me.

I walked out the door and all I could think was; "I have truly lost my mind!"

I couldn't stop thinking about the fact that I was probably going to go to jail or worse yet, prison.

The only things that I still had in my life; everything I have ever worked hard for; like my career; all the college I had done, and all of the things I had accomplished in life.

Would be gone too, just like all the people that didn't want me around.

Because of 1 night of drinking way too much whiskey and God knows what else, I was about to sink to a whole new level of low.

I had never been to jail and I was proud of myself for usually choosing to be the angel.

Usually, in spite of how hard life been for me, I was eventually able to take the higher path and love life anyway.

I couldn't stop thinking about all the things I had easily overcome through the years over and over and over!

But this time, the Devil must have taken over in my conscious absence. I had let my guard down way too much and now I would regret it for the rest of my life!

All of my hard work and dedication to being better than my upbringing. All of the years of doing my very best to be a good role model for my children. Every single good characteristic that I worked hard to maintain.

It would all be gone now. All of it … gone and my perfect record of never going to jail ruined!

Because I thought it was a good idea to stop listening to my gut and live recklessly.

What in the hell was I doing? What in the hell was I going to do now?

The thoughts would not stop spinning through my mind like a hamster spinning the wheel.

I went back to my van and I called the phone number that was on the piece of paper he gave me.

A woman answered "Hello?"

"Hi there, are you with a girl who got injured at a party last night?" I quietly muttered.

"Yes, this is her Mother. Who is this?" she replied.

I paused. Took a deep breathe, and said, "I am the one who did this to her. I need to turn myself in!"

I began to cry uncontrollably. I had truly hit rock bottom!

"Do you have any idea what you have done?" she asked.

"No! I truly do not, but I will take full responsibility for it. I have heard enough. I am so sorry for what it is worth ... I don't know what happened!" I cried

In that moment, I couldn't help it. I could feel the woman on the other end of the phone having complete compassion for me.

I wasn't sure why, because I had injured her daughter with my bare hands. I was so ashamed of myself.

In that moment, I felt surrounded by Heaven for the first time in months. I felt like I had angel wings wrapped around me; tightly.

I wasn't sure how, but for some reason I knew it would all be ok ... I just felt it.

The girl's mother asked me to please come to the hospital and meet with her to talk.

"Yes ma'am, I will be right there!" I said.

On the drive over there, I felt peace, love and the element of compassion all around me; unexplainable, But there!

I sat with a woman I had never met before that day, for hours.

We sat outside the hospital on a bench as she listened to me and my story. I wasn't sure why she even cared; but for the first time in a long time, I felt heard and understood.

She asked me if I was ready to go see her daughter and I bravely stood up to go face my ultimate demon right in the face!

Right after I finished visiting the girl who I had unintentionally but yet intentionally harmed;

I got down on my knees and prayed for her and for me and for everyone in the entire world that day!

I wasn't sure why, but the girl's mother walked outside with me and we sat down on the bench together one more time.

The girl's mother held me tight, comforted me, and gave me the most compassion I have ever been given.

She told me that she forgave me and that she had so much respect for me that I owned up to what I had done.

She explained to me that she was going to let me off the hook; only because I showed up and apologized.

She said she would let it all go, but only if I promised her 1 little small thing.

"Anything!" I said.

"I will do anything to be given a second chance to make life right again!" I said to her with strong conviction … and I meant it truly and deeply … I knew I had to be done with this reckless behavior … For good!

She grabbed my face in her hands and she cried; and said, "I cannot explain any of this to you, because I do not understand it myself; but, do you believe in Jesus?"

I stood there in complete aww of the Universe; crying and shaking.

I said "Yes! Yes! I absolutely do!"

She then explained, "I am not a Christian or even religious woman. To be very honest, until today, I wasn't sure if I even believed in anything. But when you called me; I could feel and see the presence of a man around me. He looked like Jesus."

I felt absolute truth in her words. I could feel her speaking to me from her very soul. I knew she had experienced an intervention.

She then said; "I heard a voice say that there was a sheep that lost her way. He said you were a very good sheep, but you forgot who you are and why you have come!"

In that moment, we both fell into each other's arms and cried together uncontrollably.

As soon as I was able to speak again, I explained.

"To be quite honest, I have been seeing Jesus my whole life. I have never been able to place my connection, but it has always been there. However, in the past 6 months since things have been dark and horrible for me, I haven't been respecting myself or my connection or anyone. I have been through so much and I truly have lost my way!"

I continued … "I promise you, I am a good sheep. I truly mean well. I haven't been treated well by others and it led me to acting up out of hurt and anger! I honestly do not know why I did what I did to your daughter, as I truly do not remember it; but I promise you, if you forgive me, I will pay it forward for the rest of my life!

I will promise to always be a better person every single day. I promise to always have compassion and give others more love then I was ever given. I promise to stop drinking until I black out and I guarantee that I will never do drugs again!"

She smiled at me and said "This is some sort of divine intervention. I can't explain it, but this was supposed to be a lesson for you. I feel it. I am supposed to forgive you if you promise to please let this be a lesson and learn from it!"

"I promise!" I said.

She backed away and then said, "One more thing. Do you have children?"

I replied "Yes Ma'am, but I had to let them go live with their dads, because I am homeless. It was the hardest thing I ever had to do. It was all because I was abused by a man who I thought loved me and everyone in my life turned their backs on me. I am stuck and don't know where I am headed in life. I do for sure though that if it wasn't for my children, I would have ended this miserable life months ago!"

She stared at me like she knew exactly how I felt.

The look on her face told me that she had walked in the same shoes to some degree; but she wasn't going to say it!

Instead she said, "Please, do what you can to get those babies back. Stop the nonsense right now and get your life back on track.! Promise me you will live for those children and never get in a situation like this again!"

I smiled just thinking about the mother I truly was. This was not me, this was not how my story was supposed to go!

I was greater than this darkness that had taken over. I knew this was a sign from above.

I shook my head and replied "Absolutely! I promise!!"

She then reminded me one more time; "like Jesus said; you are a good sheep and you are not that far off track! Someday, you will look back at this and know it was a page turner for you!" she lovingly said.

Before I could answer her, she stood up and walked back into the hospital doors.

And as I watched her walk away, I knew I had been visited by an angel once again, channeled through that woman!

I had been here before several times. I know what that feeling is that you feel when you are being guided by Heaven.

I had no choice anymore. If I wanted to make a difference in this world, then I had to straighten up and stop feeling sorry for myself!

I knew I was being told to be a better version of me than I had been being lately and clean up my act!

No one deserved to be treated badly! Not anyone, ever!

I heard the calling, I felt the message, and I knew that this was a true Miracle!

I decided in that moment that I was always going to be thankful for the blessings and love I received that day!

I would appreciate this once in a lifetime "get out of jail free" card!

Yes, this would be the turning of a page. I would walk the line from this day forward; helping anyone that I could possibly help.

I would make it my life's mission to always pay it forward!

"Thank you, God," I said out loud; "Thank you Jesus!" ... "I hear you; loud and clear and I promise to change my ways!"

For the next month, I went to work and then slept in my van. I stayed away from everyone and everything in hopes that I could change directions in life.

I started saving every penny I made, so that I could get a place to live.

I knew that if I just stayed focused, I would continue to go in the right direction. As hard as it was to be all alone, I knew it was what needed to be for me so that I could get my life and my children back!

I figured, it shouldn't take me long to have a place to call home. I needed to just keep going!

From that day forward, that is just what I did. I was done letting darkness take over! I was done letting others ruin my good intentions! I was done being so badly misunderstood!

I decided that no matter what it took, I would find a way to make others understand me and see the real me!

32

CHAPTER

Hey Soul Sister

AFTER BEING SHAKEN to my core for far too long, I had finally turned onto a new path of self-love and practicing peace over war in every area of my life.

I realized that I didn't need anyone to save me, because I learned to safe myself.

I spent a lot of time dreaming and planning how wonderful life was going to be as soon as I got my own place and could be a full time mom again!

But it seemed that the harder I tried, the longer it was taking. It was costing me more money to be homeless and live in my van, than it would to live a normal lifestyle where I paid rent and bills like everyone else.

I started to become a little bit resentful again, because I felt like I didn't deserve to be living this way in the first place.

Days and nights went back and forth in my mind between feeling thankful that I had a good job and all of my basic needs were met; to entertaining thoughts of how far I had already gone; only to take what felt like a million steps backwards....and I started to lose hope.

Just when I got to the point where I was starting to get a little frustrated with the progress not moving at the speed my ego wanted it to; just like clockwork ... as she always seemed to do, my big sister Tammy soon became my saving grace yet again!

It was like she could just feel it when I needed her. She always seemed to enter my life just in the nick of time.

I got off of work one Friday and Tammy called me. When I answered the phone, she asked, "Hey girl, I haven't talked to you in a long time. I wanted to see if you are ok?"

"I am not ok! How did you know?" I said

She paused for a moment and said, "Well I called your mom to get your phone number and she said she hadn't talked to you in a very long time!"

"Well, I am homeless and living in my van. It's a long story!" I said.

She was always stern with me and I heard her conviction when she said "I don't care what happened, it's time to come stay with me for a little bit. Come see me!"

I began to cry uncontrollably, and I said "ok! I am on my way!"

Now, up until that point in my life's journey; I had such a sense of not ever belonging in my biological family.

I had a deep inner feeling of being energetically alone and unloved. (besides my celestial friends who showed up on and off throughout my life).

But, in that moment, when I was met with so much understanding and love from my older sister, was absolutely completely thankful.

In that moment, for the first time in a very long time, I felt completely loved by a family member.

I had always heard it said that love can heal all wounds; And I am pretty sure it does!

Because that day when I walked through her door, my big sister Tammy lead me to the best hug I think I have ever received from anyone.

Her and I sat down in her basement that night and had the best heart to heart and soul to soul connection that I have ever had.

Her with her Diet Coke, and me with my Coke!

We smoked cigarette after cigarette together and just talked.

We talked about everything and everyone and she ended up lecturing me on what she thought I was doing wrong in life!

I had no choice but to agree with her, because she was the big sister and had lived more life than I had.

She gave me advice and love like I had never know that night. After she was done giving me my licks and kicks, she got up from her chair and strolled across the basement floor.

Just when I couldn't see her anymore, I heard her call out to me, "Come here"

I looked over and saw her lay down on a little futon couch/bed she had in the basement and motion me to come lay beside her.

We both laid down, side by side; laying on our backs looking up at the ceiling; talking about everything from the Universe to what we loved to eat.

That night would end up being the first time in my entire life that I felt like truly I fit in somewhere within my blood family.

I told Tammy; "I don't know why it is, but for some reason, I am not meant to feel like I have a blood family. I have plenty of blood family members, but not one of them seem to understand me."

She replied "Oh honey, you belong with me! You have always belonged with me. You are my only sister, my one and only sister. You are my soul sister!"

And then she added, "Do you not feel that?"

"Feel what?" I asked.

In that moment I had a quick thought that maybe she could feel and see the things I could, but I didn't want to speak of it and be wrong.

I sat there, anxiously hanging on her next words; waiting and hoping we were even more alike than I had dreamed of.

"Tell me, little sister, do you feel that Energy between us?" she answered.

There was a pause ... a silence ... a moment when we both looked each other in the eye and no words were spoken.

I knew exactly what she was talking about. Yes, I could absolutely feel it. I was always able to feel it! Even when I had hurt her in the past through my own innocent stupidity as a teenager.

I felt unconditional love from her like no one else had ever shown me and even when she was mad at me, I could feel it!

So, Yes, I could feel that energy and vibe between us!

Before I could answer her question though, I needed to know what she knew about me that she wasn't saying.

Maybe for the first time in my life, someone else will be like me!

"Tammy?" I questioned.

"Yes love?" she answered

"If I tell you something that no one else knows about me; will you please not judge me?" I asked

"I will never judge you, no matter what! You are my baby sissy!" she exclaimed and hugged me so tight.

As she pulled away from the hug, I made a very brave confession to her.

I laid there on my side, and she on hers, facing each other as I bravely spilled my guts.

I said, "Ever since I was a little girl; I can see things that others can't.!"

"Really?" she said with excitement

"Yes, and I can feel people's emotions. It's weird, I can always tell when others dislike me or when their love is true.!"

"Oh, my love is true!" she exclaimed

"Yeah, I know, but this energy you speak of … Between us …" I mumbled

"Well, I just …" I tried to spit it out but the words weren't cooperating with me.

She interrupted me, rolled on to her back and gazed at the ceiling in her basement; and said,

"Say no more! I know exactly what you mean. It has happened to me my whole life too!"

I couldn't believe what I was hearing. I said "Really?"

She continued; "Yes, but I just have ignored it my whole life. I can feel such a strong connection between you and me though. I felt it since the moment I saw you all those years ago. I knew you and I are connected on another level outside of time and space! I bet even when we die, we will still be each other's sisters!"

"Yes!" I yelled out

"Yes! We most definitely have a different connection than I have ever experienced with anyone! I can't explain it, but it's there!" I exclaimed.

She continued to gaze at the ceiling and said "I used to see beautiful little angel like spirits around my bed when I was little, but after I saw my little brother dead, they just went away! I think because it was my fault he died!"

I watched her as she broke down. Suddenly, tears began to fall down her face and I asked her, "What happened? I am sure it was not your fault!"

"Well, you know that we have a brother in Heaven, right?" she asked.

I was in shock at how fast our conversation turned from how beautiful our connection was, to another sibling that I had never heard about.

"No … I did not know that!" I said.

"Yeah, his name was Davie. He was the cutest little boy I had ever seen when he was born. My first baby brother. He had very big blue eyes and I would have done anything for him!"

"Oh wow …" I answered in between her sentences.

"Well, one day I was asked to watch him. I was told to take him outside to play. I wanted to play hide and seek. I was 8 and he was 2 and I told him to hide and I would come and find him," she continued on…

"I went to find him after doing my counting, and I saw the garbage dumpster tipped over. I knew in that moment that something very bad had happened!" she explained as she began to cry harder.

"I am so sorry Sister!" I tried to comfort her. I tried to take the pain from her held her tight.

She then said "By the time it was all said and done, I knew it was my fault he had the accident. I was supposed to take care of him and I failed miserably! Ever since that day, I have never been able to forgive myself!"

I held her tighter. I knew her heart did not deserve the hurt she was carrying.

"Tammy?" I asked

She pulled away from the hug and quietly whispered, "Yes?"

I could see an angel behind her of a little boy. in fact, it was the little boy angel that I had seen on and off throughout my life.

He was back! I couldn't believe my eyes.

I heard him say he loved her. I heard it loud and clear. I asked my sister; "You know that Davie still loves you and that he is your guardian angel now, right?"

She looked down and then looked me straight in the eyes and replied "Without a doubt. yes, I do believe that!"

"You no longer need to carry that Burdon. It was an accident and you were just a young girl!" I said.

"And ... that is why I love you so much!" she exclaimed.

"You just have some sort of gift that makes people around you calm and healed. It's like you are Magical. I never felt comfortable ever talking to anyone about that. I can't believe I told you in detail what happened. It feels so good to get it off my chest!"

In that moment, I felt so in love with my big sister and I felt so thankful to be in her presence.

I lovingly replied, "Well, you are the one who saved me! You took me in when no one else would give me the time of day. That means so much more to me than you will ever know! We have healed each other here tonight!"

I made the decision that night that no matter what, I was always going to be ok, because I had at least 1 person on the earth that loved me unconditionally. Even when I wasn't perfect, my sister still loved me!

I also decided that I would do whatever it would take to not only be a good person (as I promised the Mother of the girl, I had injured a few months prior); But I would stay connected to whatever that heavenly guidance was that always seemed to come in and out of my life.

I started to wonder if maybe I truly did have a gift of heavenly Connection that others didn't have?

Because many times throughout my life I had heard others tell me "I never felt comfortable telling anyone before but I felt compelled to tell you!"

And "I can't explain it, but you have a very comforting and peaceful energy about you. I just feel calm even talking with you!"

I started to notice more and more that I would end up in situations where others needed help and I was always in the right place at the right time to assist.

I really started to tap into my intuition and allow it to lead and guide me like I did when I was a child.

Life started to ease up a little bit for a while.

I started to see that when I would follow my inner compass, life would bring me true blessings in all ways!

I started to see that I had a higher calling; but at the time, I still had no idea what it was.

Waking up from the Illusion (Age 31-40)

33
CHAPTER

Turning the page

I HAD BEEN living in Beaver Dam for around 6 months when I finally got my own apartment and really started putting the puzzle pieces back together after a life of complete shambles for so long.

I was really starting to feel proud of myself again. I had overcome some very bi obstacles time and time again and although this last one almost became the death of me; I knew that I had to go through it to learn and grow and become me!

I had a great job in Madison but had decided to permanently stay in the area where my Sister lived.

I mean, why not? I had her, and her Mother, who had really become a surrogate Mother for me too in the absence of my own mom.

Also, because of getting close with my Sister, I also became close with my brother from another mother Ernie who was not my brother by blood; but more of a brother to me than any of my blood brothers were at the time.

In fact, he became one of my best friends! We were like the 2 misfits (but in a fun and loving way).

He was also a 70's love child who really never knew his Father and we bonded over that so much.

On holidays that year, neither of us had anywhere to go, so we celebrated together; just the 2 of us!

Ernie and I went everywhere together. We were always laughing and finding ways to make even the most frustrating things funny.

I finally felt like things were back on track.

I was on my way to having my kids come and live with me again.

I had a family who loved me; even though they weren't "Blood".

My career continued to get better and better. I was climbing the corporate ladder and gaining great momentum doing it!

I ended up getting a job at the Walmart distribution Center in Beaver Dam working in accounting for a while; and then eventually started school again to get my Nursing degree as I missed working in the medical field.

During the time I lived in Beaver Dam, I made so many true and real girlfriends (who I am still close with today).

Life was back on track and I started to see my "Friends" around my bed again at night.

I Joined a church while I was there and that too became a strong piece of who I was.

I did everything I could to help others when they needed me, and I upheld the promises I made to be a productive part of society!

I took on a job of bartending on weekend nights when I didn't have my kids and was so very proud of myself, because I did not drink at all. I stayed sober and had a blast doing it!

I never had the need for alcohol or drugs anymore, because I was high on life!!!

I met a man that I felt a very strong connection to, and he and I became very good friends right away.

For a couple of months, he would ask me out, but I wasn't sure if I wanted to see anyone, because I was still trying to get my children back and I wanted to walk the line!

People were very drawn to me during that time in my life and I could see people's auras and energy flowing in and out of their beings.

I could see angels everywhere all around the town. I was in the flow of my own divinity more than I ever had been before.

I just kept it all to myself, as I didn't need any reason for my life to be goofed up again.

I didn't need anyone knowing that I was different!

I would never share any of it ... Not a chance!

But just as quickly as things seemed to be on the upswing ... Life once again started to take a few turns that I was not expecting!

As usual, as soon as I felt life flowing, a storm would roll on in!

My health was on the decline, and I was in excruciating pain.

My Degenerative disc Disease was progressing fast and hard and I was starting to lose function in my legs.

I was having panic attacks daily and very badly. It seemed as though when I went into Walmart and other big stores, I was almost guaranteed to have one.

I didn't really understand at the time what was happening. All I knew was that I could feel that dark cloud trying to block the sun again.

I sensed that life was about to take a devastating turn. I just felt it but couldn't explain it.

But in spite of all of it, I just kept plugging away; doing my very best to stay on track and do everything I could possibly do to be a good person.

I wanted to prove to myself and everyone around me how good of a person I was.

I began doing everything I could for everyone around me.

I started to spend too much time and energy and attention to those around me.

Although I didn't recognize it at the time, I was going too far with my promises I made to that woman in Madison at the hospital that day.

I was giving myself away (and then some) day after day!

But I knew that I had made a promise to myself and to the lady in Madison and to my higher guidance that I would live the rest of my life serving others, no matter what!

The problem was that I forgot I had to serve myself too.

In January 2008 I finally gave in and started an exclusive relationship with the man who I would end up spending the longest relationship of my existence with and some of the hardest and greatest years of my life with.

I had no clue what life was about to throw at me that New Year's Eve when he asked me one more time if I would please be his Girl.

I knew by the way he never gave up on asking me out all those months, that he would be a dedicated Man.

Little did I know, just how dedicated he truly was.

I usually never introduced any of my boyfriends or dates to my kids in those days. After the experience that they had with Satin, I swore off any Man being any sort of influence in their lives except for their own Fathers.

But I had no reservation about introducing them to my new love. He had an immediate bond with them and within a couple of weeks of dating, it already felt like we were our own little family.

I had not had this kind of vibe in such a long time.

I felt a strong sense that all of us were being prepared for something bigger.

I could not put my finger on it, but I had dreams of a grand staircase almost every night. In the dreams, the staircase would come down and I would climb up what looked like a stairway to Heaven.

Every single time, I would get about half way up and I would see my angel baby brother Davie, along with another small little boy sitting there, looking lost like he needed a mommy.

Each morning when I would awake from that dream, I would wonder if another child was about to come into my life.

Even though I couldn't have anymore children physically; I had a strong and overwhelming feeling that I would become a mother to a 3rd child; a little boy.

I was excited, because at that time, my children were back living with me full time and I was more than ready to do this family thing again!

34
CHAPTER

Another devastating blow

ONE THURSDAY EVENING, I called my brother Ernie and asked him to come see me at the bar when I was working.

I wanted to tell him all about my new-found love. This one was different. This time it was special.

I wanted him to meet the man who I finally let in after so much time.

Ernie was my brother and he was my protector at that time.

Ever since I started working part time at the bar, Ernie would sit at the end of the bar all night and wait for everyone to leave.

Ernie and I had an agreement when I was bartending; I gave him free drinks all night and then would help me clean up afterwards; every weekend!

I loved having them there and he loved being able to make sure no "Dirt Balls" (as he called them) could lay their hands on his sister!

This particular Thursday evening, that I texted my brother to come and see me, was on the cusp of Super Bowl Weekend.

Ernie came down and walked in the door with a huge smile on his face.

"Hey, you!" he hollered across the bar.

"Hey ... You!!!!" I answered back. We always said that to each other. We had a bond that no one else could understand!

"Guess what?" he said to me as he walked up to the bar.

"Chicken butt?" I answered back again; as I grabbed a pint glass and began to make him his favorite drink.

"No! seriously. Stop making that drink! I am sober! Are you proud of me?" he asked me with great excitement.

You see, he had an addiction to drugs on and off for years and had recently decided that he was going to get his life together too, just like he saw me do!

Ernie and the mother of his young child, Stewie had struggled with addiction for a long time.

They had their home raided several months earlier and Stewie was taken away and sent to a foster home.

I had asked him several times, "Please let me adopt my nephew!"

But Ernie just kept promising me that he was going to stop using and get his son back, even if it meant that he would have to leave the love of his life to do it!

So, in that moment, I looked him so deeply in the eyes and I saw that he was sober. I knew he was in fact sober, because his eyes were clear and bright!!!

"I am so very proud of you brother! Here is a nice crisp glass of water to celebrate with!" I exclaimed.

I ran from behind the bar and he ran to me and we hugged and laughed!

I meant it too. I was so proud of him; he was going to do what he said he would do.

Just like he had told me he would, he was taking the first steps to getting his baby boy back!

I mean I knew what it was like to not have my children living with me full time.

I understood the shame and embarrassment of not living with your child; however, I could never imagine what it would be like to have my child taken away and sent to foster care.

"Yes!" I thought

"You did it!" I said.

"Let's celebrate!" I exclaimed.

"Yes, I want to! But I have to go for now. I just wanted you to see my face and know that I truly am on the right track! I will text you tomorrow and we will get together this weekend and celebrate with food, since neither of us are doing drugs or alcohol these days!" he said.

"Great! I will make us food then! Call or text me tomorrow!" I replied.

I will never forget how brightly he shined as he smiled and walked out the door.

I spent the next 2 days playing phone tag with him. Back and forth!

For some odd reason, we were not meant to get together that weekend.

I listened to a voicemail from him Sunday evening and he told me how much he loved me, but he was going to hang out with friends that night.

He told me if I wanted to, I could come to the bar and watch the Super Bowl with them; but I was already home for the night and decided I had plenty of time to spend with him the following week.

I did not know it would be my last opportunity or I know I would have chosen very differently.

I went to work Monday morning at my regular job.
Around 9:45am, my desk phone rang.
I answered it.
"Good Morning!" I said.
"Hi there, it is your sister … Tammy. Will you please leave work and go to my mom's house?" she asked
"Ok, but why?" I said.
She seemed very annoyed and said, "Little Sister, please do not make me tell you over the phone! Just please excuse yourself from work for the day and meet me at my mom's house! ok sister?"
I felt every piece of my being shuttering. I felt like I already knew what happened, but I didn't want to believe what my gut was telling me,

"Tammy …? Who is it about?" I asked
"It's about our brother Ernie" she said,

"Please just come home to my mom's!" she pleaded with me.

I just couldn't leave it alone. I just had to know.
I cried out, "He isn't dead Tammy! There is no way he is dead!"

"Yes, unfortunately, he is! Now please, please just listen to your big sister and meet me at my mom's house!"; she raised her voice and I knew I needed to stop with the questions and just go.

I hung up the phone and I fell out of my office chair. I hit the ground and fainted.

I don't remember a whole lot of the rest of that day, or much of the several weeks after his funeral.

I had to come to terms with the fact that the one person in this world that truly understood how it felt to be abandoned as a baby and feel like an outsider in every family situation in the world; would never share another moment of time with me.

The person who I shared my Holidays with when everyone else had invites!

The person who I had encouraged with my own story to change his life!

The one person who I cherished with everything in me was gone … Just gone!!!

I truly just couldn't understand life anymore!

I truly just had enough at that point! I mean will life ever stop kicking me down?

Why? Just why?

I later found out that the weekend when I was playing phone tag with him; he had gotten together with his son's mother to celebrate his birthday.

Against his better judgement, she had talked him into doing drugs one more time for good measure.

Once more time to celebrate his birthday and then they would both get sober and get their son back!

Unfortunately, since he was sober, and he used the amount of Methadone that night that he would have used when he was using; his body wasn't used to it anymore … It was too much … it took his life!

I cannot even tell you how mad I was at myself for not going to meet him for the Superbowl festivities that night.

I felt like I could have changed the outcome. Why didn't I change the outcome?

Before I could even begin to try to process what had happened; everything in me knew I had to do what I had to in order to get my nephew!

I called the county and they told me unless I was married, there was a small chance in being able to adopt any child, ever!
I was just devastated! Defeated…. once again!
Here I was, once again in a pit of hell!
As soon as life gets good, that ever-loving dark cloud just has to appear and let me know it is still hanging out!

I just didn't understand … why? Why me?
I laid in bed and screamed at the top of my lungs that night "God … Why do you hate me?"
My heart was just crushed, beyond devastated! How was I going to stay in the light this time? How would I work through the very deep grief that had engulfed my whole being?

35
CHAPTER

New Family Unit

THE NEXT DAY, my new boyfriend came over to visit and said, "If you need a husband, I will marry you!"

I was tempted, but I felt like who was I to marry this man, so I could adopt a child. Would that be fair to him?

"You know that means you and I will be committed to raise this child forever, right?" I said.

"Yes ... I know that. If it would save a child's life, I will do it!" he said

"We don't even really know each other!" I exclaimed.

"I know, but we will get to know each other very well if we raise this child together!" he said.

The next thing I knew We were married, bought a beautiful home on the lake and were in the process of adopting a beautiful baby boy who needed parents!

Life seemed to be back on track, and it was a long process, but Stewie became our child within a year after that,

In fact, we had all of the kids. My 2, his son, and Stewie all living with us full time.

The more life came together, the more it seemed to continue to fall apart though.

My health continued to decline, and I started to lose my eyesight 2 years later in 2010.

I ended up having to quit my job, because I could barely get out of bed in the morning. I could barely walk.

With all of us living together, my new husband and I and the kids, it felt like I finally had found that "Family" I had been looking for all those years.

I was just happy to have a family and that I was still walking the line.

I was being a good person and loving my family. I volunteered any chance I could get to try and bless someone else; even though my own health was fading very fact!

It wasn't long after the adoption of Stewie that my own mother began to reach out again after all that time.

Slowly but surely, I started to regain my relationship with the original family that I grew up with on the farm.

My Husband and I and the kids became an everyday part of the Farmer's Market that my parents who raised me owned.

It was like I was a brand-new person who had a brand-new life and a brand-new chance to re-establish an ultimate connection with a brand new part of my mature, adult self.

I was reconnecting with everyone in my life that had ever mattered to me and I was peacefully existing with each of them.

The only person I wasn't peacefully existing with at the time was myself.

My health continued to decline and the people who I had in my life didn't seem to notice.

I had to quit Nursing school as it got bad.

All my dreams were once again slowly slipping away from me as I once again was secretly in silence planning on how I would exist when I couldn't barely get dressed anymore.

The next couple of years, we moved to Poynette to be closer to my Parents and the farm and eventually, we grew further apart from the family I had in Beaver Dam.

A couple of times Tammy and I would see each other, but it wasn't like it was before.

I was torn because although I was back in at the farm; the people who had been completely loyal to me all those years didn't think it was a good idea for me to be close with those who had hurt me so deeply just a few short years prior.

But it was different at that point, my Mother hadn't had a drink in years and my dad was sober too.

Their main focus was raising vegetables and running the farmers markets and my main focus at the time was doing everything I could to be a part of it all.

I truly wanted to make every effort I could to finally fit in within their family!

I wanted so much to be a part of both families, but then the other part of me wondered how I could be so selfish as to not be thankful for what I had.

I had the love of the parents who raised me and the approval of them too.

Well, not completely, but it was enough for me!

As long as I was working on the farm with them, they would accept me and love me. Or so I thought.

Until one day I was introduced to a customer by my dad as my Mother's Daughter only.

And all I could think was "I thought I was your daughter too!"

I think that about crushed me, when I realized that no matter what I did, I would never be fully accepted again by the man that I wanted love from the most.

Neither of my fathers accepted me for who I was.

For a short time after my brother Ernie passed away, my biological Father came into my life again too.

But it would end abruptly when he called me up one day out of the blue, drunk and said "You think you are so cool. don't ever contact me again!"

To this day, I honestly do not know what happened, but according to him, I know what happened and am lying about it.

I had no choice other than to just be thankful for the relationship I had with the man who raised me.

Even though he would never completely accept me; he at least accepted me enough to work beside me in his fields and to work for him.

All I knew for sure was that I never wanted to be without my family again and I would never let any man or person Come between my Mother and I, ever!

It wasn't long after moving to Poynette that I started really seeing and feeling things strongly. I started to really have strong dreams and intuitions about people and circumstances.

With my health declining so fast, I tried really hard to ignore it. I didn't want chaos again.

All was ok with the world for now, but as I always did, I started to feel that dark cloud approaching.

36

CHAPTER

Health Scares

ONE DAY I went to Beaver Dam and saw Tammy.

She told me that she had been having trouble with her back and that her doctor had been prescribing narcotics to help with the pain of the Degenerative disc disease she had (just like me).

It was crazy watching both of us decline so fast. I tried to help her, but things just went very wrong between her and I at some point and I decided to stay away from her for a while.

Around that same time, I was having panic attacks almost daily; I wasn't working anymore at all, due to my health.

I was very sick ... mind, body, and soul.

I figured all the years of trauma were finally catching up with me.

But, no matter what, I kept up my hard work helping others, paying it forward and spending energy that I truly didn't have to spend.

My connection to what seemed like another realm of existence seemed to get stronger and stronger and although I continued to ignore it ... it was strong ... I just couldn't anymore.

The more time I spent at the farm where I grew up, the stronger the connection to Nature (or whatever it was) became.

Life was extremely crazy back then. It seemed like everywhere I went, there were people and situations that were speaking to me on a much deeper level than ever before.

I had this insatiable urge to grow herbs and study plant medicine.

I wondered if I was supposed to use it to help my health. The thoughts were overwhelming at times.

One day I went into the Doctor and told him "Listen, I need you to please help me. My life is being affected very bad here and I am losing function in my legs. What else can you do for me, as I cannot lose any more of my bodily functions!"

The doctor looked me straight in the eye and said "Look here, you just need to get used to the fact that your future will be built around narcotics and wheelchairs! There is nothing more we can do about it; your spine looks like broken train tracks!"

I said, "How long do I have until I will be in a wheelchair?"

"About 5 years or so, I am sure you will be completely incapacitated; give or take a few!" he replied.

I will never forget driving home that evening and sobbing … Wondering why? Just why?

What did I ever do so wrong to continue to be faced with adversity?

I could feel that dark cloud so strong. I sensed that life was about to take another devastating hit.

I couldn't shake it. I tried to ignore it, because I had work to do. I could not get consumed in nonsense.

Trying to make sense of life had become a losing battle for me. I just figured I was supposed to keep being punished.

Otherwise, why would life keep getting pulled out from me whenever it got good?

I had tried so hard in my life to be a good person. So, why is it that the people who don't really care about others seem to skate though life without troubles?

While people like me that truly wanted to do right and wanted to make other's lives easier seemed to take all of the punches and kicks?

A few months later, I started losing my eyesight and started a 2-year testing for M.S.

With my health on the decline, and my soul calling out so loudly to me to hear it speaking to me, I felt like I was going out of my mind.

I continued to work side by side with my dad in his fields, making deliveries to stores and being everything, they wanted me to be!

September 20, 2012 was the day things changed substantially once again.

That morning, I got up and went to the farm to pick my mother up to go to a doctor's appt. with me.

When we left that morning, my dad came outside and wanted to know if I could come back later and help him pick pumpkins in the field.

I told him yes, I would do that.

We went to the doctor and then I dropped my mother back off. She got out of the vehicle and Dad walked up to the door and leaned in through the open window.

My daughter and I were in the car … He said, "Why are you wearing a towel on your head?' to her.

"She said because of Mom's Cigarette Smoke; I don't want my hair to smell!"

"He leaned in a little bit further and looked me straight in the eye and said, "Tell your Mother to quit smoking!"

I will never forget it and if I had known that those would end up being the very last words, he would ever speak to me; I would have come back with something really good!

Later that evening, while in the pumpkin patch, he died suddenly; doing what he loved the most!

37
CHAPTER

A New Level of Existence

THE STRANGEST THING happened to me almost immediately after my dad passed away.

I still don't know how to explain it, but it seemed like after I lost him, I really became connected to that which was unseen by others.

It was like his death would move me into the next level of my existence; and he seemed to have some sort of an attachment to the "Awakening".

I could not explain it, but I could feel him around me all the time.

I could hear him speaking to me,
but at the time I thought I was imagining it.

It became as strong as it was when I was a child again.

It was uncontrollable any longer.

I had angels around me everywhere I went and the more I ignored it, the more it would try to get my attention.

My appetite to make and sell herbal medicine became so strong.

I started eating healthy, using herbs, veggies and fruits to heal my physical body and I was absolutely amazed at the transformation my body started to have.

I began meditating to help with the panic attacks.

I enrolled in Herbal Medicine School, because the calling to heal myself and others had overcome my very existence.

I started making a few little salves that I sold at a local rock shop once a month along with a few others who did readings and called themselves "mediums".

When I was there, amongst all of the mediums and healers, I felt at home, and I felt like I was supposed to be there (can't explain it).

I had no clue what I was getting myself into, because I had little to no knowledge of what they did or why I needed to be around them; but the need to learn overtook everything about me.

Little did I know at the time that these people were my "Soul" family; even though at the time I had no clue what that meant.

All I knew was that they seemed to know me more than anyone ever had!

They knew things about me that I didn't even realize.

The girl that invited me to sell my stuff there called herself a "Shaman".

Although I had never heard of a shaman before and had no idea what it was, it resonated with all of my being.

Even though at the time I couldn't figure it all out; for the first time in my life I felt like I was amongst people who were part of a whole different league of Human Beings; like myself.

I didn't know why I fit in so well, but yet, I knew that I was not meant to understand it quite yet.

So, I just went with it and enjoyed getting to know who they were and who I truly was.

Somewhere within my being, I felt as though I was about to graduate from some sort of soul initiation.

I felt it with everything in me. I knew that I had a higher calling and I knew that these new-found friends of mine would help lead me to the right path.

Even though I was not experienced with the things they were and even though I felt like I lacked the Universal ancient knowledge to be amongst them; they were enthralled with me and seemed to just honor my presence.

I had never been loved like that before and I figured there must be some mistake.

These people think I am something very special; but do they know that I am not perfect? Do they know that my own parents do not really want me?

I prayed they wouldn't see the real me; but at the same time, I wanted them to see all of me too!

One day I traded some skin healing salve for a "Chakra rocking" (AKA balancing). I wasn't even sure what Chakras were, but I trusted this lady "Sherrie" for some reason.

She knew all about my Father in Heaven and she said she could feel him around me. She told me he was with my dog I grew up with and she described the dog to a tee.

I couldn't explain what happened when she was "working" on me, but I felt the energy moving into the top of my head and circulating through my body.

I could feel it strongly.

I saw angels and sparks of light all around both of us.

I couldn't deny it any longer, there were angels trying to connect with me and speak with me.

But this time, I wasn't the only one who was seeing it and feeling it.

I finally was amongst others who had experiences like me, and they fully believed in every word I said when I would speak of my experiences.

Sherrie and I both saw and felt the Angels that were trying to communicate with me that day.

Ok, Ok, Ok ... I said to myself and to the angels.

"I will allow the connection!"

Now I do not know for sure what exactly she did to my energy or my aura that day, but it was never the same again.

That night, as I was falling asleep, I saw my childhood dog standing beside my bed.

I mean, I had seen people and things around my bed my entire life, but it hadn't happened like this in many years.

Had she opened a portal to another dimension? I still didn't even know what a Chakra was?

Just as I rolled over, there he was; standing at the end of my bed in plain sight ... My dad!

I was startled and woke my husband up ... "My dad is standing at the end of the bed" I exclaimed.

"What?" he said

"Please ... wake up ... I just saw my dad standing at the end of the Bed!" I yelled again.

"Oh ok ... that's nice!" he said.

He just simply didn't understand. I was either connected to things beyond the veil or I was going completely nuts!

The next few weeks were completely profound, as I began to see spirits everywhere again.

I saw them walking in and out of houses and people around me, but this time was different ... I was no longer willing to keep my mouth shut about it ... I felt like I must share!

I could not keep this lifelong secret quiet any longer, as I was convinced that I was not imagining this anymore!

It would be confirmed by a popular psychic Medium (Molly Morningstar) a month later that my dad was standing at the foot of my bed that night. She called on me out of everyone in a 100 people crowd.

My dad had "Come Through" and confirmed things through her that made myself, my mom, and my Daughter all true believers for the first time in our lives.

But I still wasn't sure what any of this had to do with me.

I was just a girl who had been through a whole lot and was on a mission to re-gain the health that I had lost through the years.

I bought a book about connecting to Angels, since they had such a strong need to connect with me, I wanted to know how I could communicate with them better.

But when I opened the book and read the first 2 sentences, it said the words "Evoke" and I about went through the roof with fear!

I was not trying to "evoke" anything!

I mean I have had a hard-enough time trying to just be a normal girl all my life.

I have tried hard to not connect with things that others can't see.

I was sure as hell not going to purposely "evoke" anything into my life!

It was shortly after that, that I received the diagnosis of M.S. from my Eye Doctor.

I was devastated. after all these years, I finally have a formal diagnosis.

As per usual, just when life got exciting, I would take another spanking!

I was bound and determined to beat this though. This time, when the dark cloud came calling me, I shook my fist at it and said "get away!"

The Ultimate Becoming of The Wholeistic Healer (Age 31 and 43)

38
CHAPTER

The Awakening

IT SEEMED AS though, the more I started losing my physical eyesight; the strong my spiritual sight seemed to be getting.

The next thing I knew, things were getting really different with me. I could feel my whole inner being changing.

Then one Saturday, I went to the rock shop for my monthly "day of light" event where I would sell my herbal salves and chap sticks and a few aromatherapies.

This time, I met a lady there that wanted to trade a reading for a tub of plantain salve with me.

She called herself "the artful medium", and she would draw a picture of the Spirit Guide she saw working with you.

I didn't really know what that meant, but I felt a strong desire to do the trade with her.

As I sat down at her table, she smiled and said, "Oh honey, you do not know what you are, do you?"

All I could think was "How come everyone keeps saying that to me?"

I mean I have heard that said from Jesus all my life, "You know not what you are", but I wasn't sure if I had imagined all the Jesus stuff at that point.

I smiled and said, "What do you mean by that?"

She leaned in to me and replied "Darling, you don't realize how gifted you are! You are very psychic; but you don't believe in what you are seeing and feeling. am I right?"

I couldn't believe it. How did this woman know this? Maybe it was a good guess?

With everything within me, I wanted to believe her, but I just wasn't sure.

"No, I am not psychic. "I said.

"why do you say that?" she asked.

"Well, I am not very sure what being psychic means, I guess. I cannot see the future or anything like that" I answered back.

She smiled a big loving smile and said "ok. Well were you raised Catholic?"

Yes!" I said

"And, you decided at an early age that you didn't believe in all the antics and politics and dogmas involved?"

"That's correct!" I said.

"I see that you have a nun around you. She is one of your spirit guides and she says that you have angels that have been trying to communicate with you for quite some time, but you refuse to connect with them; Out of fear maybe?"

I couldn't believe it.

How did she know all of this? I knew that there was no way she could be guessing on some of what she told me.

She said with conviction. "Your guides are telling me that you saw your dad standing at the end of your bed, and you bought a book on how to communicate with angels; but, were terrified and didn't end up reading it.

"Also, you have a son who almost died as a baby several times. He is very special and gifted too.

You also have a daughter who is a crystal child as well. Is any of this connecting for you?"

I was stunned. I opened my mouth to speak, but nothing would come out.

Before I could reply she said "Ok. Jesus is one of your main guides in this lifetime and he has been walking beside you your entire life. He says you know this and have seen him and spoken with him many times throughout the years; but you seem to think you are imagining it, because others have told you it isn't real!"

At that point I wasn't sure whether to be excited or very creeped out by how much she knew about me.

She continued. "You are in a spiritual awakening Hun; you will soon know exactly who you are and why you are here! They are telling me that you love Holy Hill?"

(Holy Hill is a very special Catholic Church about 2 hours away from my home where miracles have been spontaneously achieved throughout the years.)

"Yes … I absolutely adore Holy Hill!" I said with so much excitement; Because at this point, I felt so much truth in this woman's words.

She knew way too much about me and there was no way that she could have been just making good guesses anymore.

She went on to say, "Ok so they want you to go to Holy Hill as soon as you possibly can. You have specific instructions here. Go to each of the stations of the cross, pray for you, your oldest Son, and your daughter. After you go to each station, go into the basilica and send honor and respect to Jesus and all of Heaven and Earth."

I sat there wondering who are "They" who wants me to do this? who's instructions were these? I was absolutely in shock, aww, and wonder all at the same time.

As the reading closed up; she let me in on a few more things I wasn't expecting.

"You are a very important piece of the great awakening that is happening on the planet right now. You don't realize it yet, but you will live an amazing life in the years ahead. I am honored that I was the one who got the privilege of communicating this to you. Please do not ever underestimate your gifts anymore; and no, you are not imagining any of it. you never were!"

All I could think was what is the great awakening and what does it all mean? It is all so much to take in.

I had no idea what she was talking about, but I had such a strong feeling like I should listen to what she said to do.

At the end of the day, I spoke with one of the people I worked with. One of my soul brothers who said to me "You see what you see! You hear what you hear, and you know what you know! Don't let anyone else ever tell you different again!"

"Ok, I said."

do you think I might be psychic?" I asked.

He smiled and said "Oh honey I know you are. You have to believe in you though. Do you believe in you?"

"Not really, I said. I have been through so much, I am just not sure what is real and what is not anymore. I am hoping it will all make sense soon as everyone else seems to be telling me it will."

I went home that day and I was never the same again.

I called my mom the next day and asked her if she would like to go to Holy Hill with me for the day.

Since there was no school at the time, the kids were free to take a road trip for the day too.

Myself, my mom, my daughter and my baby boy all headed out to Holy Hill shortly after that; we planned to spend the rest of the day there.

If I would have known how the day would go, I would have probably planned it a bit different.

However, if I had known what was about to transpire, I am sure it wouldn't have happened!

But it did happen. It was something out of a story book! It was miraculous and something that I never ever expected.

We arrived at Holy Hill that day and it was late Fall; it was beautiful, and the weather was just about perfect. Very warm for Mid October (10/11/12).

I had no clue at the time that there was a significance in the date.

We walked over to the stations of the cross and I knelt in prayer at every single one. I prayed for my family, for the Earth, and for all of existence.

As I walked to each station, I tried to imagine a situation in my life where I could connect the particular station to a circumstance where there could be forgiveness and / or healing.

I used it to the best of my advantage. and I was pleasantly surprised at how much I had forgotten that needed forgiving in my life.

My oldest Son was almost an adult at the time, but he and my step son had put us through 2 years of complete teenage hell with their shenanigans.

I was concerned that my child would overdose and die like my brother had several years earlier.

I was terrified of drugs and alcohol at the time, due to my experiences with them and what I had watched my entire life happen to people.

I prayed hard that my young sons would see the light and clean up their acts ... the stress at home was out of control and my marriage was on the rocks, due to the extreme amounts of issues we had with the boys.

Things hadn't been that great for a while.

I just wanted peace, serenity, healing and happiness!

After I left the stations of the cross, we walked the property and then walked up to the doorway of the basilica.

2 mourning doves flew past my head. I had never seen them up close before, but these beauties were definitely there to greet me. I certainly felt it.

They cooed and tweeted at me, as if to welcome me to the next level of my existence (although at the time I didn't realize it).

In fact, I felt some things I couldn't explain, as I walked up to the huge doors of the cathedral. I felt like I was lost in time, or maybe walking in between worlds. dimensions really; but there still to this day is no way to describe it in human language.

I walked up, opened the door, and was greeted with the most high and holy feeling I had ever felt.

It was a feeling I could never describe or explain; but if ever there was a feeling of being greeted by "God" or the highest of highs, then this was it!

I said "Wow, do you feel the holy spirit in here mom?"

"Yes, there is some sort of shift in here, I feel it too!" she replied.

"Wow, I just can't explain the feeling in this Chapel!" I exclaimed.

I watched as my oldest child and my youngest child looked around in wonder at all of the decorations and amazing features we were walking in to.

I gazed with joy at my Autistic son as he seemed to be completely blown away by this place too.

Although it was my first time there, I felt very strongly like I had done this walk many times.

We walked all the way up the isle and as I learned when I was a young girl (it came back like riding a bike); I knelt in genuflection, made the sign of the cross on my chest, and then we all found a spot to kneel and pray.

We all sat in silence for a few moments.

Suddenly, I saw a light flashing out of the corner of my eye and I looked over to the right just a bit.

There was a beautiful statue of Mother Mary and then I could see what appeared to be an Aura around the statue.

I rubbed my eyes a couple of times; thinking that my eyes must be foggy from having them closed in prayer.

I tried to focus, but the energy was strong, and I began to feel it connecting with me.

I felt an overwhelming sense of peace, calm, and like all was so completely right in the world!

I heard a voice say, "Look to the left!"

I swore I must have been losing my mind. What in the world was going on?

I tried to resist looking left, since I figured I was "Imagining" things again; I tried real hard to ignore it, but the calling was so strong and I was overtaken with wonder.

I turned my head and saw a little nook off to the side, which harbored a statue of Jesus.

I saw 2 nuns knelt on the floor in front of the statue and the more I tried to resist it, the stronger the pull was for me to get up and go over there.

I leaned over and whispered to my mother "I am going to go over by the Jesus Statue!"

She nodded her head and I got up and wandered over to the left by myself,

As I stood up, I felt that electricity or aura; some sort of strong energy that was radiating off of Mother Mary pull me inside.

I still can't describe it any other way, as it was like I was in another world for just a few moments in time.

I walked up to the statue of Jesus and bowed my head in respect and love for the Savior.
Just as I began to pray, I watched at the statue seemed to come to life.

I watched the hands outstretch and point towards me and I thought I must be losing my mind.

As I backed away a bit out of being completely startled, I heard a voice say, "You are a healer, heal as I do!"

I fell to the ground instantly, overwhelmed with so much emotion and energy and just completely feeling everything all at once!

As I lay on the ground, I saw my entire life flash before my eyes, and I was shown every single thing and situation in my life that had led up to this.
People, and places, and circumstances that I had always wondered about, Completely confirmed to me as I saw it on what seemed to be a sort of screen before me.
In that moment, I knew exactly who and what I was and why I had come to Earth.

I saw glimpses of what I think were other lifetimes I have lived that have all added up and brought me to this point in time.

I saw scenes that showed me lifetimes of living on a Native American Reservation and being a "Medicine Man",

I saw a peek of a young girl foraging through wild plants in the jungle".

I saw a High Priestess in what appeared to be Egypt, who was having Aromatherapy treatments of that time done for me.

I also remember seeing myself standing on a beach in what looked like and I felt was Atlantis; I had Blue skin and I was a very profound Goddess type of person.

Then I saw a flash of a lifetime living in the woods in a tiny little cabin; I was a Native American Woman who was married to a lumber Jack looking man.

For a brief second, I then saw myself doing hands on healing in a shrine or temple where thousands of people watched in adoration.

Suddenly, though, like a flash it went to a time and place where I watched myself get hung alive and I received the feeling of people trying to shut me up!

And just before I came back to reality, I was shown a prairie and a dress I was wearing in the 1800's (looked like Laura Ingles time frame) and imagine this; I was making medicine for the local pharmacy.

I thought to myself, how can this be? Since I had declined the Catholic faith all those years ago?

Shouldn't I be punished for not obeying? For following what I felt deeply inside?

I wasn't sure what was happening, but I felt like I was being blessed beyond measure in that moment.

Maybe this was pure validation that everything I have ever felt deep inside was truth. More than I had ever known.

I continued to lay on the ground, completely crippled with humble gratitude for what had just happened.

In an instant, I heard my mother say "Hey, what are you doing? Why are you laying on the ground?"

"Mom! I just saw Jesus!" I shouted

I sat up and before I could say another word, she exclaimed, "Get up, you are scaring your kids!"

I interrupted her again, because she didn't seem to understand me; maybe she didn't hear me.

"Mom!!! I saw Jesus!" I repeated.

She looked at me sideways and said with conviction "Yes I know, there is a statue right there, it's beautiful!"

I knew she had no way to comprehend what had just happened to me; hell, I didn't even know how to comprehend it!

I tried once more time; "No Mom, I saw Jesus come to life! He spoke to me. He told me that I am a Healer."

"I heard him say it, outload!" I explained.

Now by this time, both of my kids were standing there looking at me too and of course I did not want to make any more of a scene than I already had for them or anyone else.

I stood up and walked out of that basilica that day and although I was sure that my family had thought I lost my mind; I knew deep in my soul that I was in my right mind more than I ever had been before!

The whole way home that day, I stared out the window in wonder at the new information that I had been given about my existence.

I spent the next week registering for herbal medicine school, writing my own care plan on how to heal my own physical body and asking a million and one questions to those I knew who had also experienced profound awakenings.

I mean, how many paths had I walked as a Human being? How many lifetimes have I lived on Earth? Why am I so special to have this happen to me?

I had so many questions but felt humbled by the gifts that began to rapidly appear and come in after that day.

The only thing I knew for sure was that within a few weeks I was secure in knowing what happened that day.

Psychosis? No way
Hallucinations? Not a chance.
Spiritual Awakening? That the lady at the Rock Shop had talked about? Absolutely ... You cannot convince me otherwise!

I know what happened to me that day. And although I had many experiences with Jesus throughout my life. this was so different; it seemed so sacred and so divine ... So Holy.

I wasn't sure which path I felt was the correct one, but I knew for sure that I was unconditionally loved by something so much bigger and greater then me! something unexplainable!

I started journaling all of my mystical experiences after that and began putting my puzzle pieces together.

Although 2 years prior, my daughter was drawn to learn REIKI healing; I had declined out of fear of what it was.

I figured it must be time for me to learn Healing on all levels in all ways.

If I was to be heavenly and holy healer; then I had great work to do so that I didn't let Heaven down.

I made a sacred promise that day to live my life as Jesus did; as much as I could, I wanted to help people heal.

I wanted to be a strong source of light in people's dark times.

I wanted to take my role as a Light Worker very serious and I would always remain humble and thankful for the opportunity to Serve in the greatest army in the universe. The heavenly army!

After everything I had been through in this lifetime … the highs and the lows … the ups and downs; one thing always remained real and true and that was my intuition and strong inner calling was always my best guide!

After what I was shown that day, I would always listen to "God" and my inner calling before anything or anyone. I would do my best to get others to hear theirs too!

I had spent many circumstances when I was younger not being the best person I could be. I was being given an opportunity to make things right; to even the score; to balance the scales!

39
CHAPTER

The Medium

I SPENT A lot of time in the next 3 years really just learning, educating myself and developing my psychic/Mediumship channels.

I still didn't quite believe that I was "Psychic" though, as I think I truly didn't know what that meant.

I had an old school belief system in place that told me it was an unbelievable thing.

What I was failing to recognize was that I was "Psychic" and gifted with being a unique channel of Heaven my entire life; I just couldn't see it underneath all of the human expectations and rules I was placing upon it.

About a month after my Awakening, I finally realized that the Light and swirling colors I always had seen when I would close my eyes to go to sleep was not just nothing.

I realized that was my divine connection and that when I would relax and just let it in, I would be shown the most beautiful visions of what my heavenly team was helping me with.

The more I would tap in to my own energetic connection, the more in tune with messages from beyond the veil I would become.

I got to the point where I started hearing and feeling people's angels and Spirit guides speaking to them through me.

I started to hear and see loved ones on the other side clearly that were speaking to people.

But I still wasn't quite confident enough to say any of it out loud. What if I was wrong? What if I was just making this up in my own head?

What if I was just Imagining all of this?

I would go through periods of extreme confidence in who I was; followed up by extreme feelings of not being worthy enough to have profound gifts.

I would feel like I was crazy at times! I would go from seeing someone's soul shining at them to not being able to feel a thing!

Once I was able to get far enough on my path where I had gained confidence and strength due to my own healings I had done on my own body, mind, and soul; then I began to do healings on friends and family members.

But, for quite a while, I was still feeling like I wasn't sure I should be doing it.

I could feel Jesus there with me every single time. and at times Mother Mary and many other heavenly helpers and light beings which helped me to feel like I was supposed to be doing it.

Every single time, people would report to me that they could feel my energy flowing through their bodies and some would feel me taking the pain out of places they suffered.

Some would even report feeling like they went out of their bodies while I was working on them.

The more sessions I did, the more confidence in myself and my abilities I began to gain.

I will never forget the first time I allowed Heaven (or what some people would call "Spirit") to come through while I was working on a client.

She was on the table and I wanted so very much to share with her what I was hearing and feeling; but I was so afraid to be wrong!

Even though I tried hard to ignore it, I sure couldn't deny the fact that I kept hearing "Adam Ant" over and over I would hear "Adam Ant".

I thought to myself. "Dam you and your imagination! Stop it. just be cool!"

But I couldn't deny it, I kept hearing a voice say loud and clear; "Adam Ant", over and over again!

Now up until this point, I was able to ignore things I was hearing and feeling and sometimes even seeing when I would work on clients.

But this time, no matter how much I tried, it was not going to go away!

"Fine!" I said in my head to the spirit that I felt in the room with me.

"Fine … I will help you communicate … What do you want me to say?'

I heard a distinct voice say. "Tell Margaret blue flowers!"

I was so confused; "No way! I am NOT going to say that!" I quietly said to the female spirit that was with me in the room.

I looked down and my client is laying there with her eyes closed; peacefully resting on the table.

I wondered if I was truly making this up. The client didn't seem to hear anything, so maybe I was losing my mind.

I had finished up her session and then, as I always did, I helped her sit up.

I sat there looking at my client and wondering if she would want me to share what I was hearing with her.

I went back and forth in my mind about a thousand times, and just as I decided I would keep it all to myself, I heard the female spirit in the room say to me very loudly, "will you please ask Margaret about the blue flowers? Please?"

I knew that responding to the female spirit in the room meant I had to ask Margaret some questions that may end up making me lose a client; but for some reason, I couldn't let this go, so I took the biggest risk!

Without further reservation, I just opened up my mouth and said, "Um ... Margaret?"

She smiled and said "Yah?"

"Well. There is an older woman here that will not stop trying to get me to speak to you for her. I have never done this before, but I am gonna give this a shot! Please bear with me!"

"Oh awesome!" She replied.

"OK well first of all she says that I am supposed to say blue flowers!" I said.

She looked quite puzzled and to be quite honest so was I.

"Ok, what about this then. While I was working on you, I kept hearing the words Adam Ant! Does the 80's rock star have any meaning to you?" I asked.

And the next thing I knew, she was saying, "Adam Ant ... A-dam A-nt ... ADAMANT ADAMANT ADAMANT.. OH MY GOD AMANANT!"

"So, what does that mean? Does that mean something?" I asked with excitement.

I was in a tizzy at this point. I wondered, was I truly performing the job of a "Medium" here? Could it be?

"Yes! It does! I mean, not the 80's star, but my great grandma's last name is Adamack! Margaret exclaimed.

Her name is Margaret Adamack! Oh wow! Come to think of it, I just left the cemetery before I came here today. I just realized, I left blue flowers on her grave!" she explained with so much excitement!
Both of us were in shock!
Oh Wow! I thought to myself; You just can't make that up! I had no clue about any of that!

I was truly developing my gifts and I would never ever again; ever not speak what I was hearing!
I learned my lesson. This was not just some imagination thing; this was truly a God Given gift that I was meant to use and develop to help others!
I must stay humble and focused and figure out where this will lead me next. I knew I had lots of work to do!

From that day forward, my channeling gifts came so fast!
I was blessing so many people with connection to loved ones; easily and without any mistakes!
The more I did the more confidence I was building.
In the meantime, I was growing lots of herbs, making medicines and I had graduated as a Certified. Master Clinical Herbalist and Certified Master Clinical Aromatherapist, I had a Masters in Energy Medicine, and started really building up my practice.
I started my own business called Wholeistic Healing and I began to really make a name for myself.

People loved me, they trusted me, and I was honored to help them on their journey.

It started to feel like I fit in somewhere in society for the first time in my life. I was a healer and it felt right. All was right with the world.

I could not ever explain it, but I finally had a place in the world.

I started to see fairies all over in my gardens. I started to feel a connection to so many different realms of life and existence. and no matter what, they all seemed to know and honor me, they all loved me!

I had never felt so loved in my entire life. I was loved by the one thing that most Humans simply didn't understand or even know existed; the Universe!

It was all almost too good to be true!

40
CHAPTER

The Blue Butterfly

THE DEEPER I went into the path of the healer; the more people and places and circumstances would show up to confirm everything was truly real.

Before I knew it, I had become "The Wholeistic Healer"; well known and loved by many.

But what no one else knew was that deep inside, I truly did not love myself; not even one bit!

I started to feel like I wasn't worthy again. Just like all the times before in my life, I felt it was about to come unglued, all over again!

I began to get an overwhelming sense of not belonging again; and even though there was no apparent reason for it, it came on so very strong!

I kept trying to ignore it. I kept trying to stay happy and be everyone's favorite healer.

I had a strong feeling like I wasn't supposed to be married to my husband anymore.

I was ashamed of myself for feeling that way, but it was strong, I couldn't shake it.

The man that I thought I would be with forever and I were not working out anymore; it was like we just lost our romantic connection and we had been more like friends for a couple of years.

As hard as it was for me to be completely honest with him, when I did, he reported to me that he felt the very same way.

We decided to separate and just be roommates until I could find another home to live in.

Then, About a month later ...

One June morning in 2015, I was in my greenhouse, talking to and watering my plant babies and giving them love.

My phone rang, and I received one of the worst phone calls I could have ever received.

My Sister Tammy was gone. She had passed away; she died in her sleep.

This could not be happening; I mean I hadn't spoken to her in several years; I didn't get a chance to say I was sorry!

I was so sorry; how could I tell her I was sorry?

I fell to the floor once again and was once again paralyzed by the loss of a major part of who I was.

I began screaming at the heavens out of shear grief.

"Why? Why? Why God? Why would you do this to me?" I shouted out loud!

"I have been your faithful servant. I have blessed and honored people! I didn't deserve this; how could you take my Sister from me; before I could say I was sorry?" I pleaded.

Just as I lay there in my greenhouse cursing the Universe; I watched as a beautiful blue butterfly flew in the door of the green house and flew up to my face and flew around me in a spiral.

I had never in my entire life, ever seen a blue butterfly in person. I was pretty sure that they were not very common where I lived.

I had been living in this area for 40 years and although I had been such a nature and outdoors type of girl; I had never seen a butterfly such as this before.

I knew very well that this was something very special!

I watched as it flittered and fluttered around me and it seemed so angelic. If ever I could feel compassion and love in a butterfly, it was in that moment.

I could feel my sister there, strongly!

I could feel her comforting me. I could hear her say "Do not cry for me beautiful baby sister of mine; rejoice for me, for I am free!"

I couldn't explain it at the time nor can I today, but that was the day when I knew my sister was supposed to be one of my spirit guides!

I realized in that moment, that she had always been one of my major life guides and shelters from the storms.

From that day forward, she and my dad who I had lost in 2012 were both with me and around me and would guide and lead me.

That summer, that blue butterfly followed me around my gardens. I knew it was her!

By fall time of that year, my heart started to beat again, slowly.

That was the summer that I really started to connect with my Earth Angel path.

I began to see angels everywhere.; although I had been seeing angels my entire life; this was a deeper kind of knowing and seeing.

I finally started to understand who they were and how they help Humans.

I could see them clearly, I could connect with them. I could speak with them and they even began to assist me when I was working on clients.

Since the gift kicked in so strong after my sister had gone to Heaven, I felt like she had something to do with the connection.

She always loved angels when she was here on Earth. Her home was always decorated in angels and her and I had such a strong connection with our higher selves when we were together.

I felt so very blessed to be walking on the path of a higher calling and I saw the world in such a different and more beautiful way, than I had ever before.

Every time I would see the blue butterfly

It was around that time that I started to feel uncomfortable co-existing in the same house with my ex-husband anymore.

41
CHAPTER

Preparing for Dark Night of the Soul

ONE AFTERNOON, I wasn't feeling well and laid down for a nap.

Although I hadn't had a vision in quite some time at that point; I felt myself leave my body and the next thing I knew I was walking that yellow brick road again.

I was met by Archangel Metatron and a group of light beings that surrounded me and told me that I would be moving soon.

They explained to me that I needed to go into the next level of awakening, so that I could help Humanity heal.

I needed to move to this new home where I would go through a very deep and dark night of the soul.

They told me that if I allowed it, I would transform like the blue butterfly; but I had to be strong, patient, kind, and love myself completely.

They told me to prepare for this.

I was absolutely terrified, and I wondered if it was some sort of bad entity that was attacking me.

Why would my angels tell me something so horrific?

I had been through enough; why did I have to have a "Dark night of the soul""

What did that even mean?

I wanted to stay there and get more information.

I started to ask questions, but I saw the yellow brick road fading and I felt as though I was suddenly falling.

I felt myself coming back to my body this time. It was something I didn't usually feel or remember; but next thing I knew, I was hovering above my lifeless body.

I could see my body laying there on the bed, and I started to panic.

I tried to move my arm ... it wouldn't move.

I tried to get back into my body, but I couldn't; I did not know how.

I could feel my energy fighting with all of my might to try and wake up!

"Wake up ..." I said to my still physical vessel.

"Why won't I wake up?" I thought to myself.

Then I thought "Oh my God, I am Dead!"

This time I must be dead, this has happened so many times, but I had never hovered over my body like this before!

I screamed, "God Please Help Me! Jesus are you here?" and instantly I felt myself drop hard into my body!

I sat up and threw my arms and legs around to make sure they would move; I sat there for a few moments and stood up.

I was so startled. What is "Dark night of the soul?" I wondered.

I got up and went to the computer and looked it up.

I couldn't believe it; it was actually a known thing!

From that point forward, I had a strong feeling like I needed to have my own home.

I also somehow knew there was someone I was supposed to meet and be with romantically.

I kept getting guidance from my angels that I was supposed to allow the next relationship that came along, even if it didn't feel right at first!

I was told to learn from it, as to not ever do it again in the future.

It would be one of the biggest life's lessons I have ever faced; but my guides told me that I agreed to go through this in order to transform into the ultimate "Healer".

None of it seemed to make sense and I couldn't tell a soul, as no one else would believe me, so I kept it to myself.

I followed the guidance I received always, so I bought my own home by myself for the first time in my life.

Even though I had some deep feelings inside of emotions and things that were not worked out yet; I knew I was well on my way to healing core wounds.

I figured, as long as I was taking care of everyone else and helping others love themselves and forgive those who had trespassed against them, then I had no reason to worry about all of my deeply hidden (stuffed down deep) hurts and struggles.

I was excited about my new life where I would be a big girl and do everything on my own.

I thought who needs a man when you are a strong independent woman.

I had everything I needed, and life was so wonderous!

I was blessed and had lots of love and support from girlfriends and the few family members I had.

Beneath it all, though my heart hurt so badly thinking about the family members who had never accepted me and those that wanted nothing to do with me.

I just couldn't understand it; I mean I was a good person and so many looked up to me; I was gifted, talented, and not to mention a heart of gold!

So those who didn't see me for who I truly was were missing out, but why was it then that I truly I felt like I was the one missing out.

I continued to carry all of that around deep inside.

I knew I had to learn to love myself completely, so that I could help others do the same.

I knew I had to accept myself, even if others who were biologically related to me weren't willing to accept me.

I was at a point in my life where I was prepared to walk forward alone if I had to; but at the same time wanted nothing more than to be accepted by "blood" family.

I sat down one day and wrote a letter to my biological Father and explained to him that I wasn't sure what went wrong, and I didn't know how to fix it; but that I had grown and matured.

I told him that I had an awakening and that he would be very proud of me for who I was.

I wrote a letter to my younger Sister and explained to her how horrific it was for me to lose my sister Tammy while we were at odds. I asked her to please forgive me for anything and everything I had done to make her not want anything to do with me too.

I hoped that each of these letters would solve that hole I felt in my heart.

I mailed the letters out and prayed they would get them and call me.

Unfortunately, neither of them called or wrote back.

It was not easy to be me. I was not like anyone else I knew. I just wanted to be accepted for who and what I was.

I had a strong need to fit in and to try and fix everything and everyone.

But since I had made several attempts at fixing things, I had no control over, I decided that I needed to let the Universe decide how those stories would go.

My heart was full of too much emotional baggage from the past and I needed to empty my cup a little bit.

I figured if I just continued being the healer and helping other hearts, that mine would eventually feel better too; so, I continued to hold all of it in and kept on working towards broadening my "Healer" legacy.

42
CHAPTER

The Twin Flame

WHEN I MOVED into my house, I was so excited since there was a fireplace.

I had never had a real fireplace before, and I planned to take full advantage of it.

The first night I stayed there, I lit a fire and fell asleep on the floor in front of the fireplace.

I did a beautiful clearing and blessing ceremony to try and perfect how I was feeling when I moved in.

As far as I was aware, this beautiful healing room with a Fireplace would take me to the next level with my clients and my own healing journey.

I was honored to be there and to walk this path!
That night, I had a very vivid dream.

I saw 2 Native American elders walking towards me; they both had black and white face paint. One with a candle and one with a feather.

As they walked towards me, the light got very bright.
I heard one say, "It's Time now Divine one!"
I asked, "Time for what?"

The one with the feather said "Your divine mission is just beginning. You will walk many paths. But make sure your journey is kept sacred and that your mission is fulfilled!"

"Ok, but what journey? What do I need to do?" I questioned.

"Remember, when the student is ready, the teacher will appear. Do not forget who you are. You know now!" I heard him say as he handed me the lit candle.

Just as I went to reach for the candle, I felt a cool breeze and he feather blew away as I abruptly woke up.

I was completely different after that, once again.

Everything around me, all my guidance and learning revolved around learning Shamanism.

It was strong ... it was a calling that I could not deny!

I was already a healer.

I was already doing healing with the angels.

I was already making Herbal Medicines and distilling my own essential oils.

I was already teaching and leading and doing "Light Working".

Now I was being called to be a Shaman; and I knew the dream was like an initiation into the next level of my healing journey.

The funny thing was though, as I learned it, I already knew it; I was already doing it!

I had the sacred ceremonies already in my head, like I had been doing it for thousands of years.

I was so humbled and honored to be walking such a Sacred path. I wondered if the next man to come into my life would be a healer too.

It would make sense, since I was so far on my spiritual path that I could never turn back around.

It wouldn't make sense for the Universe to align me with someone who wasn't like me, I thought.

I was excited thinking about how powerful that would be to partner with someone who understood me.

Maybe that is why I had to leave my last marriage; because although my husband was always loving and supportive, even he didn't understand me.

I wasn't going to grow if I had stayed there; maybe that is what the angels were trying to tell me.

With my new level of existence showing itself to me very clearly at that point, I was sure that whatever was meant to be for my highest calling, would show up soon.

I felt a strong feeling of a new love entering my life. I kind of wanted to be alone a little longer, but deep inside I knew that wasn't meant to happen at this point in my life.

Then one night, about a month after I settled into my new home, it happened!

Just as I had secretly prepared for, the prophecy predicted several months before was suddenly upon me.

It's funny how they say a soul mate will leave you feeling complete and a twin flame will strip you of all that you thought you were as to send your soul through its highest evolution of deep seeded lessons in a fast amount of time.

Little did I know how true this was about to be for me!

Due to all the soul mate type of love and support that I had received from my ex-husband from all those years that we were together and raised the children, I had built my confidence in myself as a lover and life partner up to a level where it had never been before.

I was in a dart league on Wednesday nights, as it was one of my favorite past times.

I figured why not. since I was single.

Besides, my grown kids weren't around a whole lot anymore, and Stewie was at his daddy's house on Wednesday nights.

It was perfect! I loved it and looked forward to Wednesday nights every week!

This particular Wednesday night, I was sitting at the table getting ready to play, when all of a sudden, a man walks up to the table and says "Does anyone want to donate to the jukebox fund?"

I looked up and when it comes to seeing energy around someone, this was unlike anything I had ever experienced.

There was such a strong connection between his energy and mine. I couldn't control how I felt, even if I had tried to; but for some reason, I didn't want to!

I was tongue tied and couldn't speak.

I went to had him a $5 and I accidentally handed him a $20-dollar bill.

He leaned in and said I "like you! Will you marry me?"

I fumbled and tripped over my own being for the rest of the night. Although I couldn't explain it, I knew this must be the prophesized man I would learn the lessons from.

Everything seemed to go very fast and hard after that night.

It was like I was thrown into a spiderweb and the more I fought to get out, the more I was entangled in his energy.

He and I started dating a few months later, he moved in a few months after that; and before I knew it I was so deep into the relationship I couldn't get out.

The energy between us was indescribably delicious at the time.

I knew immediately that this was the relationship that my guides had told me about!

It was undeniable.

They told me to be strong and true to myself; but I had no idea this would end up being the best and the worst several years of my life all at the same time.

This man had a control over me that I couldn't explain.

It wasn't like he controlled my every move, but yet energetically he did.

Every rule I had ever created for myself in terms of what I would or would not put up with in a romantic relationship seemed to be trumped with this man.

All the boundaries I had set for myself after the abusive relationship I had in my late 20's to early 30's seemed to repeatedly be over stepped with this man.

It was the strangest thing, because my inner being was trying to say no, but my heart and soul outranked everything, every single time!

When he decided he was moving in, I didn't want him to as I wasn't ready yet, but was too afraid of hurting him,

I talked to my Soul sister "Sissy" about it and explaining that it was too fast, but I didn't want to hurt his feelings.

I never wanted to hurt this guy's feelings. I wanted him to feel loved like he had never been loved.

I felt so strongly that was part of why I needed to be with him. He was very wounded from his abusive childhood and he was very immature emotionally.

I placed myself so deep into making sure that he was happy and had all of his needs met, that I often forgot about my own without knowing I was even doing it.

I was tested beyond what I thought I could handle with his son who had never really been parented who also ended up moving in with us full time.

I dealt with letting this child get away with things that I never even let my own child get away with; because I also felt how much the child needed my love.

My home went from peace and calm to a literal shit show; quickly!

Every time I would try and resolve and issue, I was met with him thinking I was the problem.

He always thought everyone else around him was the problem.

This man was so good at his mental mind games, that he could make me feel like I was the worst person in the world, just by simply trying to communicate my feelings with him.

It quickly went from magic and being so in love that we couldn't get enough of each other, to name calling and put downs every time I spoke to him.

This was not what I had bargained for and I knew this was not the kind of romantic relationship I wanted to stay in for my own good.

He was more disrespectful to me than any man had ever been, and I was paying for everything most of the time.

He seemed ok with just paying some of the bills some of the time, when he felt like it.

Between playing Mommy to him and his son, one day when I couldn't take it anymore!

The crazy thing was that this man acknowledged and knew that he had this broken piece of him that was wounded from the abuse he went through as a child with his own stepfather.

One moment he would admit to me that he was taking the PTSD out on me, by blaming me for the troubles his son had; which were clearly formed way before I even met them.

But, then in the next breath, he would rage on me and accuse me of abusing his son when I would try to teach the child discipline and how to follow the simple rules of a household; just the same as I did with my own children.

Although, I knew that I was not in this relationship by accident and that I needed to figure out how to help this man and his son heal; one day, I just felt like I could not take the adversity any longer!

His son had been acting up and laughing at me when I was trying to talk to his father about his actions; but he, like usual, didn't believe me and was avoiding it at all costs.

I told him to take his son and get out! I had snapped, and I did not sign up for this!

I was living in someone else's hell that they were creating in my home for me and my son.

My child had never been exposed to this type of life before, as his daddy and I and his siblings had always lived a pretty low key, low drama type of life.

I couldn't figure out for the life of me, how I could have allowed myself to go so far backwards in life.

At that point, the only thing I knew was that this was not where I wanted to be. I decided that no matter what my higher calling was, this was not going to help me continue on my path to peace within.

I was losing faith in myself and my dreams fast. I was losing all the confidence I had gained in the past 10 years in being a good woman all the way around.

His spiderweb went deeper than I had even originally thought it did. He had spun me in so many directions emotionally that I wasn't even sure who I was anymore!

I wanted him out! Out of my life, and out of my house!

I wanted my happiness and serenity back and I knew it would not happen with him there.

He had gotten really good at convincing me how awful of a person I was.

But, in spite of me being strong that day and putting my foot down; standing up for what I felt was right; I ended up being manipulated into letting him stay.

I decided to give him another chance, since he had never been loved properly. I felt it was my job to help him heal.

I figured if I took the high road and showed him higher love, then maybe he would wake up and see me for who I truly was finally; instead of what the wounded child inside of him thought I was.

A week later he proposed and even though I knew better, I married him; because I didn't want to hurt his feelings.

I talked to "Sissy" about that too.

During the time we were together, in spite of all of the chaos and negativity; somehow, I fell very deep in love with this man.

I loved him like I had never loved another; it was unexplainable!

The biggest struggle for me after I got engaged to him, was that he continued to doubt me, he didn't believe a word I said, even though I had never lied to him!

The Energy of doubt is so strong that I didn't realize how much it was making me doubt myself!

I mean, this man doubted everything anyone said to him; mostly because, he didn't trust or believe in himself!

Due to the things he had been through in life, he was skeptical of everything and everyone!

It ended up being very emotionally taxing on me, since I began to be programmed to please him and do things his way!

He was very good at mentally manipulating things to make a sensitive empath such as myself feel guilty or like everything was always my fault.

It was your typical twin flame (narcissist/Sensitive Empath) combination.

Before I knew it, I was wrapped up as the fly in his spiderweb and about to be swallowed whole.

Our marriage was not even close to loving; in fact, I became toxic too and it was tumultuous!

On top of the emotional differences we had, spiritually, he would end up being the biggest challenge I would ever face on my Journey.

He was atheist and didn't have any sort of belief in anything other than what he could see with his own eyes and even that was hard for him at times.

So, after being within his clutches for a while, I started to truly doubt myself too!

I doubted my path and I even began to think I was extremely messed up in the head for believing in my awakening; because he was pretty convincing that I was crazy!

He had absolutely no respect for me, my path, my work I did, or my dreams!

Everything and anything to do with our relationship revolved around him and his wants and needs. although he had a twisted way of making it seem the other way around.

He made me doubt who and what I was in levels of hell realms that I didn't think existed for me anymore.

He was more than happy letting me pay for everything a lot of the time.

It was funny because up until I met him, I had never experienced anyone doubting me as a healer; but because of all of the doubt he instilled within me, others started to doubt me too.

I started receiving hate mail online. People who thought I was "of the devil".

I started getting "Blocked" on Facebook from groups and posting videos.

The negative energy in and around him was affecting every single area of my life and I knew it; I felt it.

Even though my gifts were coming in very strong and I had angels showing themselves in my videos online; I still wasn't sure if I was making all of this up as he had me so out of sorts.

I got to the point where I was ready to give all of it up; just so that I didn't have to deal with the resistance I had to face day to day in my own home.

43
CHAPTER

The Re-Awakening

THEN ONE AFTERNOON, I was home alone and really wondering how I was going to continue living this double life.

It just didn't feel authentic to me to share everything about myself anymore!

I wasn't sure if I wanted to share anything at all with the world anymore!

Although I had built this healer path for myself and I clearly had beautiful gifts to share with the world, I felt that it wasn't worth sharing or even being the Wholeistic Healer, if it meant it would continue to make him think I was crazy or weird!

The only person in the entire world that I longed to share myself with was him!

I wondered if maybe I should give up my spiritual path, then I could go back to being a normal girl, so that he would be more comfortable.

Everyone in the entire world seemed to see me for the beautiful person I was, except him!

How could it be? Why wouldn't he believe in me? I know he loved me to the best of his ability (well I thought he did at the time).

I sat there letting the mind monkeys take me on a very low path of resistance and fighting through thought after thought after thought of confusion in trying to understand everything.

Why would God (or the Universe or my soul) send this man on my path at this point in my journey, I wondered.

Because, as far as I was concerned, I had come such a long way in my healing of my mind, body, and soul before I met him.

What was this all about?

I mean, before I met him, I was so sure of myself and my intuitions and my path.

I felt so confidant in my aspirations to be a very unique healer who would channel my gifts to the entire world someday (I felt so deeply within that I was headed in that direction before I met him)!

So, it made such little sense to me that everyone around me could see me and feel me and believed what I said I felt and saw and heard; except the one person who I wanted to see me and feel me and believe in me the most!

Honestly, that morning I truly began to distrust everything too.

Maybe he was right; maybe I truly was making this all up?

I wondered if all that I had ever been through and all that I had become was really just my imagination as I had always been told as a child.

Maybe this was a sign from the Universe. Maybe this was what my higher guidance was trying to show me?

I mean, I was such a sign follower.

I bet maybe I truly was making this all up; maybe I truly was imagining all of this!

I had been here before, where I doubted everything. but not like this!

This man had a hard-pressed way of spewing words at me that would cut my bones and strip my walls down to nothing, until I was a pile of mush.

But then just when I thought I couldn't handle any more of the mind bending, he would twist again and fill me up with loving and encouraging words!

He would fill the sugar bowl up again and then I had no choice but to feel as though I was the problem!

This continued to happen, time and time again! It seemed to become the way of life for me that no one knew about but me.

But on this particular day; I knew I was being asked to truly look at the deeper meaning of my existence!

It felt like a sort of initiation into the expansion of my own consciousness

Even though in those moments of doubt, I did not see it very clearly.

I did not feel it.; in fact, all I could feel was doubt and fear and the strong need to break free of the clutches of how trapped my spirit felt.

I decided to meditate and try to come to a balance of peace within my being.

That day would end up being the very first time that I was completely encircled by heavenly Hosts and angels of light in my home.

As I lay there in meditation, I could see the light in the room lighting up bright; even with my eyes closed.

I not only saw it behind my eye lids, but I felt such an overwhelming presence that even to this day I just cannot describe.

Just when I could not stand it any longer, I opened my eyes and I saw the most beautiful angelic Energy surrounding me, the chair I was in and the whole entire room!

I sat there, leaned back in my chair and just sobbed.
The emotions I felt were so strong!
It was the highest, most Holy light I had ever encountered; even though I had most definitely experienced Heaven surrounding me many times in my life; this was completely different.

After I sat up, I watched as it dissipated into nothingness. I had a strong thought that I should video tape myself speaking of my experience.
I grabbed my phone and turned the camera on and started recording.
I lost my emotions in the video, because I was still struck with so much awe inspiration from what had just happened to me!

I shared the video on social media and within a matter of 20 minutes someone noticed that there was what appeared to be angels behind me and at some point, my dog growled and then a large flash behind me of pink energy!

It was undeniable, you could not deny what everyone was seeing with their own human eyes!

I felt so humbled and lucky that it had happened to me! I felt my spirit coming back to life.
I felt the truth of my soul again and I knew that I was receiving a life line from Heaven.
I knew with all of my being that this was no accident or coincidence. I was losing myself and the human part of me needed validation in the reality of my path.
It was granted, without a doubt!

For the first time in my life, others witnessed what I had been seeing with my own two eyes my entire life.

I came back to life with an awakening within an awakening that day!

The Video ended up going viral and got lots of attention!

It made many people truly believe!

It was so beautiful and at the time I had no clue that the events that transpired that day would end up becoming the "Norm" in my life after that.

From that day forward, I began truly seeing, hearing, and clearly feeling my guides and angels when they were around!

From that day forward, I completely believed in angels!

Although I already had experienced the presence of angels many times; the doubt that the Man I lived with had poisoned my mind into losing my connection for a little bit.

After that happened that day, there is no one that could ever convince me again that I was making this up!

I mean, so many people saw what I did that day!

After that day also, angels started to show themselves in my live Videos that I was doing to help people heal.

For a while, I was doing videos several times per week, giving readings and healings and just connecting and sharing my love, my soul with the public.

It felt wonderful to have so many people look up to me and trust in me and know the real me!

The biggest trouble I had though was that even though he saw it with his own eyes that day and several other times, he still denied that it happened.

This man still refused to allow it to be real and it continue to be a huge struggle for me.

I was living in 2 different worlds and having to stifle myself when I was with him as to not creep him out.

If he only knew all of the things I saw and heard around him, but I could never share!

Things continued to become increasingly hard between him and I.

The more I connected with my soul; the further away I felt from him.

CHAPTER

The Level Up

WE HAD A wedding coming up and I knew I should not marry this man, deep within my being; but I was terrified to face how I truly felt, so I kept letting it roll out.

After we got married, it took 2 weeks before he started to accuse me of abusing his son.

This man obviously had forgotten who he married. It was just awful.

One day I laid there in bed and wondered what this was all for.

How could it be that I could be in this type of a relationship?

I head healed so much within myself in the past several years; and I had learned from my past.

I just spent years with a man who fully and thoroughly believed in me; even though he didn't quite understand my awakening, he trusted me!

Why was it that this man who I loved more than life itself didn't trust me?

Why couldn't he see me for me?

He was the one person in the world who I wanted to please more than anyone.

But I just couldn't comprehend it; why wouldn't he believe me when I told him the things that I was going through?

It was about 6 months after the first time I saw the room light up with Heaven's love for me and my path that we had a very popular series of Celestial events that happened (August 2017) which ended with a complete Solar Eclipse.

Everyone was talking about it.

Everyone was excited for this "Eclipse" that would bring "Big Change" to the planet according to all of the popular spiritual teachers and leaders that I knew and trusted; and I felt it too.

I felt big changes coming. I couldn't explain it, I just felt it.

That day, I will never forget; I went into a shamanic meditation that morning and before I knew it I was having a vision quest.

I saw myself walking through this tunnel of light; and at the end of the tunnel, the light got very bright and wide!

I heard a voice say to me "Blue Jay … Blue Ray!"

It was the strangest thing, because in the recent months I had a Blue Jay that seemed to be following me around.

I can never explain what happened that day, but during the Eclipse, I felt my physical body morph into a different frequency.

I felt DNA activate within myself.

How do I know that? I don't know … I just knew!

After that day I was shown clear signs that I needed to explore the path of a "Blue Ray Empath".

Although I had never heard of such a thing, it was the one thing which would come to show me more than ever before who and what I was and why I ticked the way I did.

It was one of the biggest alignments I have experienced.

I was excited and all of my spirit longed to tell my new husband, but I knew he wouldn't believe me or understand.

From that day forward, my hands-on healings became so profound that people would go out of their physical bodies and have what seemed to be grand adventures when I would work on them.

Many were reporting that they felt the presence of angels, assisting me with their healing sessions.

I would tell them which angels were there and they would confirm it was what they felt too.

I was so humbled and grateful for the very unique gifts I was developing.

The more my energy and luminous body was expanding, the more profound healings my clients and friends and family were experiencing in session with me.

My spiritual abilities were exceeding anything that anyone could explain.

I have never known anyone with the strong gifts I had.

I could easily take people's pain away with a touch.

I became strong medical medium where I could tell people exactly what was going on in their body.

I could tell them what was wrong and why, and it was validated that I was correct time and time again.

People that were coming to my home to have healing sessions with me were experiencing and seeing the animals, nature spirits, butterflies, dragonflies, and pure bliss that seemed to be all around and within me.

Everyone that came would see the magic all around my house and within my entire being.

Friends and family and clients noticed how the creatures of all kinds and shapes and sorts were drawn to me and my light; the would point out to me how all of nature seemed to want connection with me too!

When I would work on clients, at any given moment, you could look out the window and see animals coming up the path to get a taste of the Holy Energy.

It was contagious and I started being called "Snow White" by those who experienced it.

People were simply amazed by me and so honored to work with me.

People began traveling to see me and I became an extremely popular and sought out healer!

When I was at healing fairs, people would gather and wait in long lines to see me!

I would send them away feeling like a million bucks every single time and it felt so amazing to make someone else's whole day!

45
CHAPTER

The Crossroad

ALTHOUGH I SHOULD have been on top of the world and it would have appeared to everyone around me that I had everything a girl could ever want...

A career that was growing fast and people who adored me and loved me and trusted me ...

I could not shake the feelings deep inside of unworthiness!

I felt unworthy to have my gifts! I felt like my husband grew increasingly disgusted with me and his doubt in my path was so strong!

I could feel it just from lying next to him at night.

We would discuss it and I would tell him "If you would only wake up and be more open minded!"

He would reply with "I am never going to believe in that. like ever!"

I realized he was never going to believe in me or my path. He was never going to believe in my abilities, and he was never going to be interested in believing in me!

I got to the point once again, where I no longer believed in me either.

I went into a deep dark depression and started to become emotionally and energetically toxic; very toxic ... Like him!

All of the darkness that I had worked so hard to hold deep down inside was seeping up.

I couldn't control it. It was like someone opened up the door to the chambers of the pits of Hell.

I realized that this man had sparked "Dark night of the soul" within my being.

I eventually realized that this was happening exactly like my heavenly guidance said it would.

It was time for me to truly face everything I needed to face, so that I could grow and rise above all the limitations that this man and the traumas, hard times, and disappointment's, all the abandonment and heartbreaks in my life had placed upon me.

Before I knew it, I was standing at a crossroads. The hardest crossroad that I had ever faced!

I knew without reservation that I was stopped at the crossroad and I knew I had big decisions to make in order to choose one path or the other ...

I knew I was being asked to make a choice. I knew Universe had presented all of the information right in front of me and I was being asked to please choose a lane!

I felt it in all of my being that I could either...

Let go of the healing path and be "Normal" to make this man happy. Be just a normal woman living a normal life and being and doing what he wanted and needed me to do.

I could give all of this up and just please my husband and those around me who thought my path was ridiculous.

I could continue to just live a mainstream life of a wife who allows her husbands wants to be what matters most.

I knew giving up my path meant giving up my career and my dreams of going global with my gifts and talents I had to share with the world.

But, giving up my path meant that my marriage would possibly get better.

Or…

I could take on the challenge of truly facing off with all of the resistance deep inside of me that was trying to tell me I couldn't!

I could choose me, truly and completely for the first time in my life.

I knew if I took the path of the healer, that I would be truly learning for once and for all who and what I was.

I knew it would take courage and strength and the ability to gather my bearings like never before, so that I could truly become that healer that would spark awakenings in others; in order to help all of humanity realize who and what they were!

I knew if I chose to believe in myself and stay on the path of the healer, I would go big, no limits, no walls and eventually, no doubts!

I ultimately, in that moment, knew that the 2 sperate lives I was living would no longer be able to co-exist.

I hadn't said a thing to him about it; but I truly thought maybe it was time to give up this alternative lifestyle I had been living and come into the "Norms" of society a little more.

After all I had been through and after all of his cruel words that raced through my mind every moment of every day….

Who was I kidding? Maybe he was right…maybe I was crazy … maybe I was making it all up … I mean people had been telling me my entire life that I was lying and making it up!

Maybe it was time for me to truly stop the nonsense and become a normal girl ...

Maybe life would finally work out for good if I could just be normal and d ignore all of this stuff that was coming to me.

I wondered if all of the adversity that kept coming into my life was centered around my strange experiences and the overwhelming need to be different my entire life.

I couldn't help but question if maybe I stopped allowing my free spirit to run the show and maybe just tamed down and remained quiet and subservient, like most people did; if my life would finally make sense after all of these years.

I spent a few days really trying to figure out which path was the best for me.

I was torn, truly torn. I wanted so badly to be able to keep walking down both paths. I didn't want to choose; why did this have to be so hard!

I kept thinking about the phone call from Hay House that I had received out of the blue, a few weeks before, asking me to write my book and publish with them!

They had heard about me online ... I was becoming someone who was well known online and in person.

I traveled all over the country doing my healing and light working.

I was so confused and torn on what was best!

I really loved this man, so much that I was willing to give everything up. if would have fixed my marriage!

I just loved this man more than anyone I had ever met, and I just wanted peace and I just wanted to please him.

If I could have known for sure that it would fix our relationship and marriage, I think I would have definitely chosen the path of being with him forever!

But, then again, there was another side of me that that was angry at him for putting me in this predicament.

I mean, before he came along, I had no chaos … no drama … no issues!

I had worked everything out in the years before I met him!

I had worked hard to gain good credit; a good reputation and I really had a good thing going for myself when I met him.

I had worked hard for it too!

Just as I would think about giving up all of my dreams and Universal gifts just to fix everything with him, I would remind myself once again that my healer path came before him!

I was so torn! I knew time was ticking and I had to make a decision soon.

I had a trip to Sedona, Arizona Planned and I figured a week away from him and home would be exactly what I needed to clear my head and see what my angels and spirit guides thought was best for me.

I figured that I had gotten really good at following signs and synchronicities and that once I got to Sedona, I could be within my own energy for a bit.

That was the one place on Earth where I would see and hear my guidance so very clearly.

I would know for sure by the time I got back whether to end my healing career or my Marriage!

I knew I needed to decide soon and either way, one had to go in order to find true inner peace.

I left for Sedona shortly after that and I expected to be able to feel my guidance very clearly while there.

46
CHAPTER

The final strikes

UNFORTUNATELY, THE DAY I arrived in Sedona, I found out my brother who lived on the streets of Seattle was missing.

We hadn't heard from him in quite a while; which normally wasn't a big deal, but he had reached out to my other brother and told him that there was a man who was trying to kill him, and then he disappeared.

So needless to say, my personal issues were put on the back burner so that we could all as a family be private investigators and try to find him!

The whole trip in Sedona, I couldn't stop focusing on my missing brother and when I got back, I was met with much more resistance from my husband.

He was not supportive at all; In fact, the more I cried out for support, the more I was met with cold hearted "Not my problem" attitude.

So, I spent some time going very deep inside myself!

Everything was a mess once again!

My life, my very new marriage, and my career (because I wasn't emotionally ok, so I wasn't really doing a whole lot but being depressed.)

I would pray and try to connect with my guides at that time and all they would tell me was that I needed to have faith and trust the Universe … All would be well.

The more I tried to trust, the more things began to fall apart everywhere around me!

I had been there before, when life seemed to fall apart around me, but this was a different feeling this time!

I truly had enough this time!

I felt as though life had been way too hard for way too long!

It seemed as though, every time I have ever thought I was done with hard lessons, I would be thrown a few more wolves to meet me around each corner I turned.

I just couldn't for the life of me understand how someone like me who was such a gifted Human being, with so much to offer the world; could continue to get myself into these situations where I had to re-vamp who and what I was!

I started to completely lose Faith in everything … I already had 2 siblings I lost to tragedy; and it was looking like I was working on a 3rd?

How could this be?

Just when my career seemed to be taking a huge leap towards broadening, it was flattened by self-doubt inflicted by the doubt of the Man who I married who honestly thought I was out of my mind!

Christmas came that year and I couldn't even celebrate.

I had nothing to celebrate; what was the point? life was messed up once again!

I wanted my husband to just love me for who I was, but by this time, he had already pulled away.

We ended up barely even speaking anymore, barely communicating, and hardly even sleeping next to each other!

By January, he walked out the door on me one morning, when he asked me for $50 and I declined because I was tired of supporting him!

I was tired of not receiving support from him. I was tired of putting his needs ahead of my own.

I was angry and I just didn't care anymore.

After 2 weeks he came back for a short time, but ended up raising his hand to me and then not coming home a couple times and it ended in a huge eruption of him in a drunken stupor after hanging out with his friends and wanting in the house after I told him "If you go don't come back" ...

I ended up calling the cops on him that night ... when I watched him get in that taxi, I knew deep in my heart that it would be the last time I would ever really see him again.

I was right!

47

CHAPTER

The Darkest Night of the Soul

BEFORE I KNEW it, that crossroads I had been standing at for the past year was gone! I must have taken too long to decide which path I wanted to choose, because, I ended up not having to make the choice after all!

The Universe made the ultimate life altering decision for me!

My husband, my twin flame, the love of my life chose divorce ... I was devastated!

The good news was though that right around the time he was leaving, my brother showed up alive!

The bliss that I felt about my brother's well being would be very short lived though.

After my new husband left, I went through what would end up being the darkest days of my life.

I was hurt, humiliated, embarrassed, trapped in my own dark pit of distain for those who had walked out on me my entire life.

I had enough of people abandoning me! How much can one soul take of being shoved aside?

Why does everyone always abandon me?

And how can it be that someone can go from feeling confidant in themselves to completely not even know who and what they are … Just like that!

I realized that I was in that "Dark night of the soul" that my guides had spoken of a couple of years earlier…this was it!

In the moments of my deepest darkest thoughts and feelings, the crossroads that I had been faced with would go a little differently than I had expected it to!

Instead of choosing my husband or my healing path, I would find myself faced with choosing to live or die!

This time I truly wanted to die!

I could simply not keep doing this roller coaster that life had me on for so many years!

I had been a really good person for most of my life!

I had done everything I could to right the wrongs I had done earlier in life and kept my promises I made to my soul and my higher guidance.

I had no intentions of ever hurting anyone; but for some reason, I just couldn't stay out of the way of other people's harm.

This last heart break hurt more than anyone ever had and I simply didn't understand why.

Was it was because I didn't get closure?

Was it because I had been dumped by a "Twin Flame"?

Was it because all of the things that I had been through in my life were finally all coming up to be dealt with?

I wasn't sure, but all I knew was that I was done!

Done with Healing, done with love, done with life!

I decided that I would end it all, because it was so much easier than dealing with the Texas size hole, I felt in my chest called loneliness and heart break!

How could I ever feel normal again after this? And besides, if I was truly some profound healer who was supposed to help Humanity with some "Great Awakening"; Then none of this should be happening; at all!

Shouldn't healers have an easier life then this?

Most healers are happy and don't have to face this pain I am feeling! Why me?

I believed I must have truly been making all of it up!

After my husband left, he sent me a few last little blows via text message letting me know how crazy he thought I was!

That did it!

I was tired of being labeled as different or weird or crazy. I was tired of being tired of being me!

I just knew that everyone around me would be much better off if I wasn't around. My own biological father never wanted me and to be quite honest, I was never fully sure if my mother did either (although she put on a good act!).

I planned my exit from this world the next day and decided I would take enough medicine to put myself to sleep so that I didn't wake up!

My siblings went out that way ... Why shouldn't I!

Every single dark thought that crossed my mind was followed up with the encouragement from my deep seeded soul wounds that had never been heard or understood.

I got my things together and I quietly planned everything out.

I figured my kids would be ok without me and I hardly had any family anyway.

No one would care ... I just knew it!

I had even reached out to my doctor only to be told I had to get on a waiting list for emotional counseling.

They didn't realize that this was 43 years of waiting to be heard and I couldn't wait ... I had no more time left!

I had to find a way out of the darkness!

It was so dark, and I could not feel my angels around me any longer.

I didn't hear any guidance and even when I was reaching for it, nothing was really coming in!

So, I set everything up and straightened up my house and got ready to go to sleep permanently!

I was just finishing up the last of the details and working on mentally preparing myself to leave this world when all of a sudden, my Soul Sister "Sissy" walked into my bedroom and startled me.

She caught me directly in the act of planning to do the ultimate act of all acts.

"What are you doing?" she cried out.

"Nothing! Leave me alone! I am just done! I can't do this anymore!" I replied.

"Sister, you weren't going to do something stupid were you?" she asked.

"It depends on what you consider stupid!" I answered back.

"No! you are Not going to kill yourself!!I won't let you. No Way!" she yelled.

"Please!!! Just let me!" I cried out.

"I can't take this pain anymore! Please just let me go be in peace!" I began to wail in pain and tears.

"Please just let me die!" "PLEASE?" I said as I fell to the floor.

She fell to the floor with me and held me in her arms with all of her might.

"I am calling all of our soul sisters. We are not letting you do this!! Ever! WE LOVE YOU SISSY!" she hollered at me while tears streamed down her cheeks.

I couldn't even speak … I just wanted the pain to stop … why did the pain have to hurt so much?

I could usually make pain stop! But this pain was more than anyone could deal with, I thought.

I made my physical body stop hurting so much in the past several years; So why couldn't I make this pain stop?

I had never felt pain like this before!

I was strong, but it was so unbearable! I wanted them to just please, let me die!

Within minutes my phone was ringing and "Sissy" handed it to me.

"No! It's my daughter, I can't answer it. I don't want her to know I am not ok!" I shrieked.

"Answer it! Here" she said as she handed me my phone and hit the answer button.

Before I could even say a word I heard from the speaker phone; "Mom? Momma? Mom?"

"Yes." I answered.

"Don't you ever think about going anywhere, do you hear me? My life would be terrible without you! I love you so much mommy! Please do not ever hurt yourself!" I heard the screams coming from my daughter's being; way deep down within her being,

I can't explain it, but something about the way her voice sounded so desperate, longing for her mom to be ok, just shook me enough to wake me out of whatever nightmare I was in!

It snapped me quickly from wanting to be dead to not ever wanting to hurt my children like that!

There was no way on God's green Earth that I could ever hurt my babies like that!

As I pulled myself out of the dark energy that had me suffocating, I wondered what was I thinking? Oh my God? ... what was I doing?

I am not sure what kind of dark energy or entity was trying to get me to leave this place that day, but somehow, some way ... Fate stepped in!

48
CHAPTER

Finally Healing the Healer

SOMEHOW GOD STEPPED in … The Universe stepped in … once again it was shown to me how absolutely needed, I am as a bright shining soul here on Earth on a distinct mission to help Humanity heal with the help of my divine team and the 144,000 other light workers who have answered the call.

That was the day that I knew for sure without a doubt (after many times of validation) that I was in fact the Wholeistic Healer and I needed to find the courage and strength to face my own inner demons that had built up, like never before!

It was time to do some true soul searching and heal my own self, so that I could truly be authentic when I lay my hands-on others.

I needed to face that which has held me captive secretly all these years.

Dark night of the soul had absolutely pulled me into a new awakening. I knew I was about to become a much larger part of the Great Awakening on Earth than I had originally thought.

The next morning, I heard an old familiar song on the radio in my car.

As I heard the words; "Aint nothing going to break my stride ... Aint nothing going to hold me down ... I got to keep on moving!"

I knew the Universe was speaking to me clearly once again.

I spent the next 4 weeks in solitude; facing myself like no one had ever faced themselves in the history of Humans on the planet!

I knew for sure without a shadow of a doubt that I was the Wholeistic Healer and that I was meant to go through every single thing I ever went through, so that I could learn and grow and overcome!

I knew I had this hard path, so that I could heal from it and hold my hand out to others who aren't quite there yet.

I faced every single Demon that told me I wasn't enough!

I faced every single Demon that told me I wasn't loveable!

I faced every single Demon that told me I did not deserve blood family members that loved me!

I looked every single Demon square in the eye that tried to convince me I was making this all up!

I smiled at every single Dark and Dense energy that was weighing me down and trying to push me off my path!

After I was done slaying the Demons and Doubts; I looked myself in the mirror and for the first time in all these years, I knew for sure who I was and why I am here!

I came back clean and clear and reassured that there is no way that anyone can ever convince me again that my path is not valid!

I broke out of my cocoon for the final time!

The final layers had been shed, and I was re-born like never before!

2 days after my soul was freed and I was in the Universal flow of gratitude for all that I had been and done...

I walked out on my porch on a beautiful late summer/Early fall day and I was admiring my beautiful gardens all around my beautiful home.

Just standing there, in so much true appreciation for the journey I have been on in this lifetime!

So thankful for the new-found courage and strength I had found to overcome extreme circumstances and always find the light eventually!

I stood there excited about how many other souls I was going to help awaken to their own light!

I thought about how far I have come and how amazing God is and just when I thought I could not get any more peaceful...

I watched as a blue butterfly landed on the blossoming sedums in front of me!

It landed and then took flight again and landed on the cedar chips I had around the garden,

It danced a little bit and then took a very short flight and landed on me.

I stood as still as I could and allowed the butterfly medicine to absorb into my entire being.

I felt it send me so much love as it circled around me time and time and time again.

I stood there in tears of joy and pure thanksgiving, just soaking in the blessings I knew I was about to receive ... Because I had done my work.

It was a great validation that I was indeed on the right path more than I had ever been before.

Big things were coming, and I was about to embark on a journey that was more magical and amazing than I could ever even fathom in my Human brain.

I thanked the Blue Butterfly ... I thanked God ... I thanked the Universe for all that I was, all that I am ... and all that I will ever be!

I have walked through the garden of Eden more than once and I have escaped the pits of Hell and if there is one thing that I learned in all of this lifetime, it is...

When you have a higher calling you feel it, see it, know it, smell it, taste it and you can even sometimes touch that which is not visible to other Human Beings!

You must have faith in yourself first ... you must follow your senses first ...

You must always follow the calling of your soul!

EPILOGUE (IN CONCLUSION)

SPEAKING OF THE calling of your soul and the Universal awakening ... returning to your own personal Garden of Eden; I decided to dedicate the epilogue of this book to the magical journey that I took to Florida to finish writing this book.

I want to dedicate this story you are about to hear to the Man who I shared some of the most magical moments of my life with and I can never ever repeat what happened on the trip If I ever tried.

I dedicate this prelude to the Divine masculine who I shared love with that day like I have never shared love with anyone.

My beautiful friend who I lovingly call "Egypt" (He knows who he is).

I began to feel the crunch coming down upon me and I knew that "Divine Timing" was upon me. it was time to get out of my comfort zone like never ever before and get this new journey started of becoming the published author that I always knew I could be.

I began feeling my angelic heavenly team cheering me on ... I could feel within all of who I am that it was time and there was no other way to explain it; I just knew it was time!

In late November 2018 I could feel all of the Earth, all of Heaven; all the creatures, people, the seen and the unseen circling around me in a sort of spotlight.

I had a dream that I was standing on top of an exquisite scene ... I was led to a huge clam shell that had been prepared for me on top of a what looked like a mountain in Sedona (red Rock).

I was told it was my throne and that I earned my spot in the light and that all of the Universe wanted to hear my story so that they could be inspired to break free of their limitations and see their truth too!

I was told that all of Heaven and all of Earth were awaiting my arrival!

I heard my maker say to me "You have earned this. You have done the work in many lifetimes. The last lifetime, you almost achieved this ... You came back to perfect your light work!"

"Beloved child ... You are the light of the world ... Go out spread light to the world! It's your time ... to take your place on your royal throne of love and light ... many have come before you and inspired you to get here and many will follow behind you in your glory and legacy!"

Now after everything I have been through in this lifetime and everything, I have overcome; I finally came to the realization mid-2018 that this was really real, and I was truly supposed to channel this divine heavenly inspiration to the world.

I had raised my hand... I wanted to spread light to Earth ... Yes!

The next day I told my daughter. "It's time!" I need to get this book finished! The people are waiting to read the words so that they can awaken and align with their destinies too!"

Although I had not shared with her about my dream, I figured it was a sign that I was to travel somewhere to finish my book. I felt like I was supposed to go "off the grid" so to speak.

I was pretty sure that it needed to be somewhere warm and tropical and most definitely somewhere with sea shells.

I told her to look for cheap flights and wherever I was meant to be would be clearly shown.

She quickly explained to me that the cheapest flight was to Tampa, Florida and that it was substantially cheaper than all other flights.

"Yep, that feels exactly right!" I said to her.

As I sat down to think about it, I heard the words "Clear Water ... Clear Channel" and I about fell out of my chair.

"Yes!!! That is, It!" I thought to myself.

I knew it was absolutely it! Clearwater, Florida was not only one of my favorite places in the whole Universe, but it was tropical and beachy and a clear channel too apparently.

As I went to bed that evening, I heard a voice say, "you need a crystal skull".

I thought it was odd, because I had never truly been drawn to them before.

I have many friends who are obsessed with the beauty and energy (magic) of the crystal skulls and they love the connection they feel when they have them.

But for me, this journey was not quite yet ready to happen I guess, because I was supposed to receive my first one a year ago and things did not align.

So, the next morning I woke up and grabbed my cup of coffee and sat down to flip through Facebook for a bit.

When I clicked on FB, the very first post I saw was a picture of the most beautiful Green Obsidian crystal skull I had ever seen.

The post said that this guy was looking for his "Guardian" and wanted to go "home".

I could feel as I read the post that I was to be this guy's guardian.

I reached out to the man who had posted it and told him my story; both of us had chills up and down our spines (little did we know that would be the first of many sets of chills we would experience).

In the next few moments we realized that I was headed to Florida and he, in fact lived in Florida too (alignment)!

We decided we would meet up and exchange energy and I knew that morning that this would become the last part of this book!

I knew it would be the final story before this book ends!

I headed to Florida a week later and although I planned on this being a trip of ease and flow, I was met with a whole lot of resistance during the whole trip!

Just when I thought I was done with soul initiations and tests and chances to make a higher choice; my trip to Florida to finish this book would end up being the most Magical trips!

Not only because of the beauty of the love and light that surrounded my being at the time, but more so, due to the darkness that was trying to ruin everything!

Yes, I said the Darkness made it magical, because of all of the growth I had this year alone!

Instead of letting things defeat me, I thanked the dark challenges for the chance to take the high road time and time again!

It started the moment I got to the airport in Chicago to head to Florida and I lost my phone at security.

The lady boarding passengers told me I had to choose between my phone or the flight.

I ran as fast as I could to get my phone and board the plane (defying everything she told me); only to then sit on the plane for an extra half hour before we took off due to an unruly passenger that needed to be removed.

Once I got to Florida; thing after thing after thing kept going wrong and the 2nd night I was hit by a drunk driver in the rear of my rental car; who fled the scene.

I ended up having to pay $500 when I returned the car due to someone else's mistake.

The next day, I received a parking ticket with the rental car, because I couldn't find the coffee house that I was looking for and stopped to ask for directions!

I went there to sit on the beach and write, but the weather was colder there than it was in Wisconsin for most of the trip!

No matter what kept trying to take my energy and gratitude away…

No matter what was trying to make me doubt myself …

No matter who was aggressive or rude or downright nasty …

I kept my head held high and I kept thanking the negative energy for helping me be stronger and rise up and over!

I knew I was being trained for my ultimate becoming and you can't get to the highest highs of Heaven without knowing, tasting, feeling, and seeing the lowest lows of Hell!

That is what Earth and being human is all about.; is it not? The bigger picture of experiencing everything that being Human has to offer us!

Well I experienced it on this trip and I am thankful for it!

But although I was terrified to drive the wrecked rental car for a 2-hour drive to meet up with Egypt.

And even though I stopped at the rental car company and asked if I could exchange the car and of course it was a no (even though it wasn't exactly safe); I knew without a shadow of a doubt that I was supposed to meet this man and share space.

I knew we would forever change each other's lives in such a massive shift.

I wasn't sure how or why, but I somehow just knew!

I had no other choice than to TRUST that the Universe had my back and would get me there safe!

Due to the financial situation I was in, because of the rental car, I no longer had the funds to purchase the skull from Egypt; making the whole thing even more challenging on both sides!

Needless to say, Egypt was given an opportunity to TRUST that the Universe had his back too!

He was given the choice to trust in me, and trust that I would pay him when I returned home and got my financial bearings after the trip.

So, even though there was so much resistance and negative forces trying to keep us apart, we both had our minds set on meeting up anyway!

The morning came and we were both like 2 small children!

Excited and both of us having a strong knowing that this was a divine mission; both of us knowing that neither of us would ever be the same again after meeting up.

I knew when I woke up that morning and the very first thing, I saw was 3 doves outside my window that I was being so guided by forces unseen to most.

I got in my car and I could feel my own divinity more than ever before; I could feel white light surrounding me, and I could feel a large alignment about to happen.

I turned on to the major highway that I would take to reach Egypt. and a van pulled out in front of me; On the back it said, "Frontier 1111".

As I felt the chills run up and down my spine, I smiled and thanked the Universe for the confirmation.

I continued to drive, and I am sure everyone in the whole world could see the smile on my face, because I was just beaming!

I stopped at a gas station to fuel up and the woman behind the counter said, "let me see your ring!"

"Which one?" I asked.

"The Om one!!" she replied.

As I gave her my hand and she glanced lovingly at my finger; I thought to myself; "Yep validation".

I thought to myself, "Om"… the sound of creation"

I have been wearing this "Om" ring for almost 2 years now and no one has ever noticed it (at least no one has ever spoke out loud that they noticed it).

I already knew I was in creation energy, but once I again, I got back in the car and smiled a big smile and said thank you to the Universe.

It wasn't too long after that, I was driving and smiling, and I couldn't stop shining bright!

On my left, I saw a Catholic Cemetery out of the corner of my eye.

Now I do not normally stop at cemeteries, not a habit I keep, but this was different. So different.

I heard my higher guidance tell me to stop in for a few moments and so I pulled in and parked.

I walked over to an area I was extremely drawn to where there was lots of statues.

I could see, feel, and hear the Heavenly hosts all around me!

I felt all of Heaven and Earth collide in that instant.

I kept walking, before I knew it, I had walked up to Archangel Michael, Archangel Raphael, and Archangel Gabriel statues facing each other in a circle.

Imagine this; they all had doves in their hands (remember the doves I saw first thing this morning? Hello confirmation.)

I gave my respects and then I walked over to where I saw Mother Mary queen of angels standing on a pillar. I knelt down and prayed.

I thanked her for all that she is to this world and all other worlds.

I cried because I could strongly feel her presence there; uplifting me and encouraging me to keep going.

I stood up and I saw a huge cross with Jesus and what looked like 4 statues surrounding him. I walked up the sidewalk towards the cross; and went to the left to see who the statues were of.

The very first one on the left was St. Luke and I almost fell over.

You see in November 2017 I had a reading from a very profound man that told me I would be finishing my book in about a year (it was almost exactly to the day when I finished).

He also told me that when I got to the last section of the book, I should call on St. Luke to help me channel heavenly grace into the book.

He also shared with me that Melchizadek was one of my spirit guides since birth and showed me a picture of him (remember earlier in the book ... the man with the white beard? Let's just say I about fell over when I saw the picture).

He said St. Luke, Archangel Gabriel, Jesus, and Mother Mary would all be leading this journey for me.

Now in my entire life, I have never seen a statue of St. Luke (not a common statue).

I felt all of Heaven cheering for me like never before.

Once again. so much confirmation and validation that I was not only on the right path; but I was about to join paths with the next level of my being (more than I would ever be able to understand in the flesh).

I gave respect to St. Luke and thanked the Universe once again. I sent love to Jesus and thanked him for all that he is to me as well.

I got back in my car and I felt like I wasn't even in my human body anymore.

As I pulled out of the cemetery, I came to a stop light and the sign on the road said "Hwy 555 this way".

I began to cry! Tears of humble honor for my soul mission.

Tears for alignment with the highest and greatest path and purpose I was on; this was what I had been working towards my entire life ... It was here ... it was time!

As I got within 22 miles of meeting up with Egypt., the GPS took me on a journey in the countryside in Florida.

I passed a river called "Peace River", which then quickly lead me to the most beautiful country roads I have ever seen.

I drove through an orange tree orchard, where each row had a different street name.

I watched as I passed "Isis BLVD" and then "Moses Road" and then "Joseph Street" (these are street names in an orange orchard, mind you.)

I watched as 3 Hawks circled me and followed my car through the grove.

Now, I typically will see hawks doing this when I am about to receive a huge blessing.

I thanked them for their presence and if it was possible, I think I started smiling even bigger.

Just when I thought the journey could not get any more magical and heavenly, I pulled up to where Egypt was parked and got out of the car.

As I walked up to him and we embraced in a huge hug, he asked me "Do you want to meet him?" and I knew he was talking about the skull he had to hand deliver to me.

"Yes!" I exclaimed. I couldn't wait!

All of the amazing experiences I had all day long, I was sure that this was going to be something very special! He pulled out the most beautiful Skull I had ever seen and handed him to me.

As I reached out to grab the skull, all of a sudden, I heard the most excruciating noise coming from the sky!

Loud ... shrieks ... sounded like yelling ... screaming and screeching!

I took the skull out of Egypt's hand and held him in my own; I could feel what seemed to be a "guardian" energy all around me.

The crazy thing was that Egypt had said the skull was looking for his "Guardian".

I was prepared to be his guardian, but the moment I held him, I knew that he was to be my guardian instead!

This Skull somehow communicated to me that he had been my guardian in many lifetimes and that he waited until I was ready and until the time was right to find me again.

I felt the truth in what was coming to me. The skull let me know telepathically that I would be moving into a much bigger soul mission after this book comes out and I would need some big "Security" to keep my energy protected!

Just as I was receiving this information, the screaming and screeching got louder and I came back to the moment with Egypt, and suddenly I said, "Let me put sculley in my car so he doesn't get broken!"

"Yes, great idea!" Egypt said.

As I walked away the screaming and screeching got even louder and more profound. I looked up and saw 3 huge eagles circling around myself, Egypt, and Sculley (my new protector had just told me that was his name).

You see, after the day I had, I would have thought that I must be dreaming, but just as I thought I might be taking this magical day to the extreme with my imagination.

Egypt belts out "Look!!!! 3 eagles!"; then in that moment, I knew I was definitely not dreaming!

Both of us watched as these very beautiful forces of Nature (not 1 ... not 2 ... but 3) circled us and screamed a heavenly screech at us ... one more time!

Wow!! We both were just amazed and we both felt so in love with the Universe in that very moment!

After the eagles flew away, we decided to get a sandwich and sit in the park and visit for a little bit;

He told me that his Peace Pipe wanted to come with him for this journey and that he knew it was time to have it activated by a Shaman.

Egypt explained to me that he felt strongly that I was meant to activate his pipe for him (as he is telling me this, I picture the Peace river that I had just passed about an hour prior ... and thought ... yep I am the Shaman you need!)

As we walked down the street to find a place to eat lunch, I watched as fireflies danced all around us and the birds seemed to cheer us on as we matched each other step for step.

We got sandwiches and sat in the park that was in the center of the town on a bench. We watched as everyone around us seemed to disappear one by one … the whole place cleared out and it was like we were the only 2 Humans in the world for a little bit.

We didn't mind though, we were so high on life at that point, that we were just enjoying the magic and each other's company!

While we were eating an angel dressed up like an elderly woman came up to us and asked us for help and advice on her journey. We both recognized what was happening and we kindly assisted her and watched as she faded away.

I could just feel the Heavenly presence. I knew we weren't alone, although we appeared to be!

It felt like we may have entered a different dimension, time, and space. I was fantastic!

After we were done eating, we went to the water and I did energy work on him. I opened his channels a little bit and then activated his Pipe though sacred ceremony.

At that park, I went to use the restroom; and after I walked away, a very strange man came up to Egypt and talked to him about his trip and how it didn't turn out how he expected it to, but he was making the best of it.

When Egypt told me this, I knew it was more validating from my guides that I was on the right track and to keep going; as that was exactly what had happened to me on this trip!

Once again, as we walked up on the beach to do the activations, it didn't take long before everyone seemed to clear out and it was like we were the only 2 people in the entire world standing there on the beach!

We talked about Atlantis and Egypt and ancient lifetimes that we feel we lived together.

We joined sacred healing space and I cannot ever explain exactly what we went through that day to another person; because, if you weren't there and you weren't Egypt or me, you couldn't possibly feel, see, or know what happened that day.

All I know for sure is that each of us activated each other to the next level of our soul's highest evolutions.

He activated and aligned me, and I activated and aligned him for the next leg of both of our journeys! It was a sacred meeting that was destiny and we both knew it and felt it!

After we were done with the sacred ceremonies for the day, I walked up to the fresh water lake we were sitting by and I found 2 small blue and green conch shells on the shore.

Now this was fresh water and they sure didn't belong there; but they were exactly what I have seen in dreams of Atlantis.

I picked them up and thanked the Universe one more time. I knew this was yet again, one more alignment; validation for both of us!

After we parted ways, I knew that an amazing new level of understanding was about to happen for both of us.

The very next day I finished my book with my Sculley by my side at a coffee shop where I sat by the window.

As I looked out said window, there was a sign outside the door for a restaurant called Sculley's! I smiled a huge smile and once again thanked the Universe for the confirmation.

Now that we have moved to the next level; Sculley and I are amazed at the connection we have to each other and the entire Universe.

After I got home, I placed Sculley on my desk and I turned and saw 4 doves sitting in the branches of the trees outside.

I cannot ever explain some things in human language or comprehend certain things while I am here in the physical world, but I have learned so well throughout this journey so far that...

When I follow the calling of my soul ... I am unstoppable, and I can overcome anything!

They say a soul on fire is unstoppable ... and baby this girl is on fire!

Strap on your seatbelt's kids because the Wholeistic Healer is about to take you all on the journey of your lifetime!

Stay tuned ... wakey wakey ... Its time!

GUIDANCE FROM MY JOURNEY TO YOURS

❖ There are people, places, and things here on school room Earth that are meant to teach you very hard lessons. The sooner you can see the beauty in these and honor them for what they are; the sooner you will find peace within.

❖ No one ... not even your blood related family members are guaranteed to love you to the level that you feel you want them to. Everyone is here to learn their own lessons and you can love them unconditionally ... that doesn't mean they will love you back ... love them anyway!

❖ Every single one of us are beautiful divine sparks of creation. Some of us feel this and recognize our divinity; others will deny its very existence. Instead of wasting your time trying to convince others of your worth you should always spend that energy helping them find theirs and then they will see yours as a side effect.

❖ There are many (many) paths that lead to the light. No matter who you are or where you are in your soul journey; please always honor the path that someone else is walking. Yours is never the only way and when we can honor someone else's beliefs and feelings it lights you both up!

- ❖ Hurt people hurt people. Even if you were raised in anger and despair … even if you have been to the pits of hell at the hand of another (even if it is your parent) please always rise above and forgive those who know not what they do.
- ❖ Be authentic, Be real, Be honest be-cause others already know the truth!
- ❖ Angels DO exist in many forms. Some of us walk the Earth dressed up like Sensitive Empaths. Never pass up an opportunity to bless another soul … you never know who is watching.
- ❖ You will never ever be loved in the way you seek to be … or find true love to the level that your soul longs for until you truly do your soul work and learn to love yourself to that level. (The love you send out is the love that is reflected back to you).
- ❖ Kindness is never wasted, love is never lost, and beauty is always present … BE YOU TEE FULL!
- ❖ No matter who tells you that you aren't … YOU ARE!
- ❖ Please stop making excuses on why you can't … because YOU CAN!
- ❖ Beloved child, you are the light of the world … go out spread light to the world!
- ❖ ALWAYS believe in what your heart is telling you, ALWAYS have Faith that the Universe has your back, and ALWAYS ALWAYS follow the calling of your soul!

BECOMING A BUTTERFLY

Have you ever watched a butterfly working its way out of a chrysalis? The process requires an amazing struggle.

Anyone who does not understand the purpose of the struggle might in sympathy snip the chrysalis.

However, please know that this would make is much easier for the butterfly to get out of the cocoon and it would be much simpler.

But, the butterfly would more than likely then be underdeveloped and never fly! Did you hear me? Never take flight.

Darling, the struggle is part of the process of developing strong wings for flight.

For so many years of my life's journey I can so much relate to the feeling that a butterfly must feel when they are trapped in the chrysalis.

A girl like me. trapped in a cocoon of people, places, situations, politics, religion, beliefs, views, and values of others that just did not feel true to me and my path and my soul's journey.

A cocoon of being held back by feelings of inferiority due to feeling other people's energy and emotions my entire life whenever I was around anyone (but believing that what I was feeling from others was how they felt about me; when in reality it was their own inner struggles I was feeling.

I know now it was so that I could help them ... but in my cocoon I didn't see that),

A chrysalis of sitting in the darkness that I felt from the world around me ... the struggle of not being loved the way I deserved to be loved, not being approved of by those I needed approval the most from, which then lead to hardships that come along with feeling like failure as a child when your parent doesn't love you and you don't know why!

A deep dark cocoon of self-doubt, hatred, disrespect because you have spent your whole life feeling like you were walking in a different dimension than everyone else around you and you have been so deeply misunderstood for so many years! You can't quite see your truth yet!

A girl trapped in a prison of not fitting in no matter where she went, not having anyone to turn to that would even remotely understand how she was feeling and what she was experiencing. A very lonely cocoon of fear that consumed to much agonizing time of self-reflection.

A girl who was so gifted with the beautiful gifts that Heaven allows Earth angels to carry in this existence; but had to keep it all inside ... trapped like a cocoon in order to try and be "Normal".

The journey to being loved was so long and hard and never-ending battles of wondering why me.

However, when the time was right ... when the wings were developed ... When the Butterfly was ready ...

She became a new and beautiful light being when she let the hell go and allowed Heaven to enter into every single area of her life and wellbeing.

Slowly ... the emerging Butterfly ... was freed ... she found spiritual freedom in learning to love herself no matter what anyone else thought of her... no matter who didn't love her back!

She was FREED when she learned to BELIEVE in herself and Believe in God.

ABOUT THE AUTHOR

The Wholeistic Healer has a very unique and amazing ability to activate other people's souls on such a deep level. A small town girl who was born and raised to inspire and heal others in ways that people just do not think of. A certified Master Clinical Herbal and Aromatherapy Practitioner, a Transformational Shaman, Master in Energy Medicine of all kinds, a Medical Medium, Angel Channel, a Reverend, a friend, a Healer, a lightworker, but mostly a master of this thing we call life! She has overcome things that would break most and has such an inspiring way of showing Humanity how beautiful the challenges can truly become with a little dose of self love and understanding. She is truly a remarkable and talented soul and her spirit activates deep awakenings for others who are ready to follow their own soul calling.